Python Programming for Beginners

Python Programming for Beginners

A Kid's Guide to Coding Fundamentals

Patricia Foster

Illustrations by Ryan Johnson

ROCKRIDGE PRESS

For general information on our other products and services or to obtain technical support, please contact our Customer Care Department within the United States at (866) 744-2665, or outside the United States at (510) 253-0500.

Rockridge Press publishes its books in a variety of electronic and print formats. Some content that appears in print may not be available in electronic books, and vice versa.

Interior and Cover Designer: Stephanie Mautone
Art Producer: Sara Feinstein
Editor: Caitlin Prim
Production Editor: Ruth Sakata Corley
Illustrations © 2020 Ryan Johnson

ISBN: Print 978-1-64611-388-0 | eBook 978-1-64611-389-7
R0

To all kids who love creating,
building, and exploring new worlds.

Contents

How to Use This Book

Welcome! As you've probably guessed, this book will teach you the basics of Python programming. But more importantly, it's going to teach you how to think like a coder!

Coders can look at big, complicated problems and break them down into small pieces, then solve each piece with a step-by-step plan. This is a useful skill for your day-to-day life, whether you're coding or not!

We'll start this book with an introduction to programming. Then, we'll cover the basics of Python and how to download it onto your computer. Remember to always ask an adult you trust—like a parent, teacher, or guardian—before downloading something from the Internet!

Chapters 3 through 9 are full of fun, hands-on examples and lessons. You'll follow along with the code and see how each coding concept can be used to build programs and games. These chapters each include three cool activities: one easy, one medium, and one challenging—all of which are perfect for practicing the chapter's central concept and your new coding skills. Each activity will end with the complete code, so you can easily follow along and check your work.

Finally, we'll put everything together in chapter 10, building a game you can play against the computer.

When you're done, check out **Code for the Road** on page 175 for ideas to take your coding skills even further.

If you run into trouble, check out **Bug Hunting: Troubleshooting Tips** on page 176. There's also a **Glossary** of common coding terms on page 181 and a list of programming **Resources** on page 180 for learning more about Python and coding.

Let's get started!

1

Welcome to Programming!

Picture the last 24 hours. How many different things have you done on a computer? Maybe you've taken photos with your phone or played video games. Maybe you've chatted with friends, downloaded a homework assignment, laughed at funny cat videos, or researched how many eyeballs an octopus has.

Computers are everywhere! And that's because computers are really, really good at one thing: doing math very fast without making mistakes.

It's we, the clever humans, who take this "fast math" and use it to solve problems. We found a way to turn math into code, and now programmers can use code to build useful programs. *How do I stay in touch with my friends?* We invent social media. *How can I watch my favorite movies without buying or renting hundreds of discs?* We create video streaming. *What's something fun I can do when I'm bored?* We design video games.

Coding is about solving problems with computers. It's about creating useful, fun, or silly programs that can make your life better. And the only limit is your imagination!

If you've never coded before, this book is the perfect place to start. Through fun examples and exercises, you'll gather all the tools you need to start building whatever games, apps, or websites you want.

1 What Are Programs?

A program is a bunch of code designed to solve a human problem. This can be something complex, like "How do I get this satellite into space?" Or it can be funny, like "How can I add dog ears to people over video chat?"

Writing a program is a bit like explaining to an alien how to go to school. The alien has never visited Earth, so they don't know what a school is, or a bus, or recess, or homework. You have to explain *everything*!

To start, you need to give the alien precise instructions to get to the bus stop: Leave at 8:15 a.m. Walk down the driveway, then turn right. Walk for five minutes and stop next to the oak tree. Wait for the big yellow vehicle.

When they finally get on the bus, the alien doesn't know how to pick a seat. What instructions would you give them? "Pick the closest seat that doesn't have two people" works. But so does "Always choose a window seat, if available" or "Go as far back in the bus as you can!"

To write a computer program or direct an alien, you break big ideas into smaller tasks. Every task becomes a series of precise, step-by-step instructions. Choices that you make without even thinking about it, like where to sit on a bus, must be questioned and explained.

The result, when translated into a programming language, is a program!

Programs might have different goals, but every program has these five parts:

- Input
- Output
- Math
- Conditional execution
- Repetition

Let's explore them!

INPUT

Imagine you're buying ice cream. Before the ice cream man makes your frosty treat, he asks you some questions, like "Small, medium, or large?" and "Cone or bowl?" and "What flavors would you like?"

Input is the information you need to start your program. If you haven't chosen your flavors, the ice cream man can't start scooping!

Likewise, imagine that you're playing soccer with friends. What do you need to get started? A soccer ball, two teams of players, and maybe a field or a big driveway. These elements can be considered the "input" of your soccer game.

OUTPUT

Output is the finished product of a program. If you order a "medium raspberry ice cream," you expect to receive a medium raspberry ice cream!

What about the output of a soccer game? The goal of each team is to win, and winning is decided by score. So, a good choice of output is the final score of both teams.

When we talk about input and output, we're looking at how the program starts and ends. At this stage, we're not worried about how we *get* from Point A to Point B. We're just trying to imagine Point A and Point B themselves!

MATH

Every computer program has a bit of math. Sometimes it's obvious. Maybe ice cream sizes are calculated by weight, and you need to divide 5 ounces of ice cream between three flavors. Or maybe you buy four cones, and math is needed to calculate the final price. Addition, subtraction, multiplication, division—it's all a breeze for a computer!

Other times, the math in a program is sneaky—you're not even aware it's doing math.

Remember that computers are fast math machines. Technically, everything on a computer—from text to images—is made out of numbers. Luckily, most of these transformations happen automatically. We don't have to worry about how a cute cat video becomes 1s and 0s through behind-the-scenes coding. We just trust that the math works.

You might write program instructions to scoop ice cream, clean equipment, and replace empty ice cream trays. But somewhere, deep below the surface . . . this all becomes math.

CONDITIONAL EXECUTION

If you ask for an ice cream cone, it'd be weird for the ice cream man to fill up both a cone and a cup. If you order pistachio ice cream, there are dozens of flavors you don't taste.

Programs are designed to have users, and different users make different choices. If you write 1,000 lines of code, maybe only 50 percent (or even 10 percent) is used in a typical day.

A program's ability to have different options is called "conditional execution." Without it, programs would be one-size-fits-all. You'd be stuck ordering the same flavor of ice cream or playing the same soccer game over and over. Sounds pretty boring!

REPETITION

Every program can be broken into a series of mini tasks. When you play soccer, you kick the ball, steal the ball from opponents, score goals, or block them. You probably do each of these actions multiple times in a single game.

Likewise, many programs do the same thing over and over. If we write a block of code that scoops ice cream, it makes sense to use that same block of code when scooping hazelnut and blueberry flavors. No sense in writing more code than necessary!

The Fundamentals

You might have heard of JavaScript, Scratch, C++, Ruby, and dozens of other programming languages.

Here's the good news: It doesn't really matter which one you learn first. After your first language, it's easy to pick up a second, then a third. Each language has its quirks, but they all use the same basic coding concepts. In other words, each language uses the same toolbox.

So, let's focus on the tools themselves, and master the coding equivalent of screwdrivers, drills, hammers, and wrenches. Once you understand how different tools solve different problems, you can build anything: a palace, a cottage, or a camping van!

In coding, the five most important concepts, or tools, are:

- Variables
- Data types and structures
- Conditionals
- Loops
- Functions

Every program—from self-driving cars to a text game of Hangman—uses these five tools. Mastering them will help you learn to think like a coder. The more you build with these tools, the more you'll understand how programs fit together. From there, you can start bringing your own creations to life! Maybe one day, when you see a big, complicated human problem, like "How do I find the fastest route from my house to my school?", you'll be able to turn it into GPS software!

Just remember, programming is supposed to be messy. All coders make mistakes. If your first try isn't perfect and your code crashes (a.k.a. it doesn't work), so what? You'll learn how to fix your code and try again. The important thing is to keep trying. Even when you make mistakes, you're learning.

These concepts are:

VARIABLES

Variables are tools that store all the information used in our programs. They're the reusable plastic containers of the computing universe! Whenever you're finished with some information, you can just "wash out the container" and use it for a different piece of data.

What flavor of ice cream did you pick? Or how many goals did you score in soccer? These choices need to be recorded somewhere. Putting them in variables keeps our code clean, organized, and easy to edit.

DATA TYPES AND STRUCTURES

Data structures are tools for organizing multiple variables. When you have a million different elements, you need a system to keep track of them all!

If variables are like reusable containers, then data structures are like fridges or lunch boxes. They make sure that no container is forgotten at the bottom of your backpack, getting gross and stinky.

Every piece of data also has a "type." The **data type** determines how much space the data needs in a computer's memory, and how the data responds to different **math operators** like plus (+), minus (-), multiply (*), and divide (/). You wouldn't use the same type of container for leftover soup and delicious brownies. Similarly, numbers, text, and "yes or no" variables all come in different boxes.

CONDITIONALS

Conditionals are structures that allow you to create a fork in your code. If the user chooses caramel sauce, they take the right-hand path. If they choose chocolate, then they go left. Each choice comes with its own consequences. Remember, users don't usually explore every piece of code. Conditionals allow us to decide which instructions are run, when they are run, and why they are run.

LOOPS

Loops are an important tool for repeating code. When you hear the term "loop," maybe you think of a racetrack or a roller coaster, something that races around the same path over and over.

Whenever you write a program that performs identical tasks, you'll want to use a loop so you don't have to write the same code over and over again. Scooping some mango ice cream, for example, probably isn't very different from scooping bubble gum ice cream. A perfect candidate for a loop!

FUNCTIONS

Functions are a tool for giving tasks to different pieces of code. At an ice cream cart, you might have one worker preparing sundaes and another handling payment. When you play soccer, team members might be offense, defense, or goalies. If people weren't in charge of specific tasks, it'd be a messy free-for-all!

Like loops, functions are ways to reuse code. They're also used to keep code clean and easy to understand. Instead of asking "What tasks are repeated over and over?" (a loop question), ask yourself "How can I break a complicated task, like playing soccer, into smaller tasks?" That's how you know what functions to build!

Talk Like a Programmer: Words to Know

Starting to code can feel a little intimidating because programmers use lots of weird words. But it doesn't have to be overwhelming!

Let's check out some common terms:

ALGORITHMS

Algorithms are a series of precise, step-by-step instructions that solve a problem. But wait! How is that different from a program?

While computer programs target big, vague "human problems" like looking for craft ideas or needing directions to the zoo, algorithms solve smaller "computer problems." These are things like "How do I multiply two really big numbers?" or "How do I find the smallest number in a list of one million numbers?"

A program often uses many algorithms. Each algorithm takes the program one step closer to accomplishing its big, vague, "human" goal!

COMPILING

Computers don't speak English, but they don't really speak Python or JavaScript or C# either. At a basic level, computers are built out of electronic switches, which can either be "on" (1) or "off" (0). **Compiling** is the process of changing the code that humans can read into the series of 1s and 0s that computers understand.

RUNTIME

Code doesn't do anything if we don't run it. **Running** code is like saying "go," and letting the computer execute your directions line by line. Picture starting a car's engine, driving it out of the garage, and going around the block. A running car isn't sitting in the garage, doing nothing. And running code isn't sitting on a page. Instead, it is actively completing its task.

Runtime is this space between starting the program (starting the car) and ending it (finishing the trip around the block).

DEBUGGING

Humans aren't perfect, and sometimes our code doesn't do what we want. Other times, it does things that we *don't* want. **Debugging** is the process of searching for the tiny mistake in our code that's making everything wonky. It might be a typo, or it might be a more serious logic error. Either way, we refer to this mistake as a **bug**. Some programmers also call these "glitches" instead of bugs, just like glitches in video games.

It can be frustrating when your code doesn't work, but you should know that even the most experienced programmers get bugs in their code! Trial and error are all part of the learning process.

SPAGHETTI CODE

When we code, our goal is to create an organized program that's easy for others to understand. You'll want to avoid making **spaghetti code**. Instead of clear step-by-step instructions, spaghetti code flips back and forth between one task and the next. Everything is jumbled together, just like a bowl of spaghetti! The program might work correctly, but it's not clear *how*. This makes the code difficult to debug. There's also the danger of undetected bugs lurking just under the meatballs!

SYNTAX

In computer science, **syntax** is the set of spelling and formatting rules for a programming language. It includes how code needs to be structured, what symbols are used, and how you need to write specific instructions. For example, lots of languages use semicolons in their syntax. Others use tabs. Each language is a little different!

Why Python?

Python is the perfect language for when you have a great idea that you want to bring to life quickly. Because it has simple syntax, you can focus on logic, instead of worrying about complicated curly braces, semicolons, or oodles of round brackets!

But don't let the word "simple" fool you. Python can do everything the other languages can and in less space. This makes Python a great language for beginners. And because it's great for beginners, lots of people know it and use it to make fun and useful programs.

Whether you want to create multimedia games or design websites, Python is a great place to start. Get ready to mix creativity and logic and build some cool programs!

What Can Python Do?

The short answer: anything you can imagine a computer doing!

The long answer is: Python is a popular language for games, websites, and data science. If you want to make adventure games with 2D graphics, Python is perfect. If you want to make a text "choose your own adventure" game, Python is perfect. If you want to get physical and buy hardware like a Raspberry Pi or MicroPython to make some electronics projects, Python is still perfect!

2

Python: The Basics

What does *installing* a programming language mean?

When you download Python, you're actually downloading a program that translates Python code into machine code. Remember that computers are just a bunch of electronic switches. The only concepts they understand are "on" and "off!"

If you want to learn a new human language, like Spanish, you'd probably use a Spanish-English dictionary. Every human language is a bit different, so each one needs its own dictionary.

Similarly, each programming language is a bit different. JavaScript, C#, C++, Ruby, Java, and yes, Python—each one has its own translator. These translators are the programs that transform code on a page into an interactive program.

Think about this: Human languages are constantly changing. Words like "selfie" or "jeggings" didn't exist 100 years ago. Like human language, programming languages evolve, too. When you go to download Python, you'll see many different versions. As a rule of thumb, go for the most recent one.

How to Install Python

To install Python on your computer:

2

1. Go to the Python website: python.org/downloads. It's always best to download from official sources. That way, you know the translator is up-to-date and you can trust the website not to sneak a virus into your download!

2. Select your computer's operating system. It's possible the website has done this for you automatically.

   If you have an Apple computer, you're probably using Mac OS X. Otherwise, you're probably using Windows. Ask a trusted adult if you're not sure which operating system you have.

   On the Python website, there are links in the banner that allow you to access translators for Windows, Mac OS X, and even Linux operating systems.

3. After selecting your operating system, you should see text that says: "Download the latest version for Mac OS X" or "Download the latest version for Windows." Under that, there'll be a button that allows you to download the latest release. Click on it!

   You can also scroll down until you see the list of Python releases. Download the most recent version of Python 3. Don't worry—since we're focusing on the basics in this book, it doesn't matter if you use Python 3.8.2 or Python 3.7.6. Just make sure the first number after the word "Python" is a 3.

4. Your click will download a package that will install Python. The package should have a ".exe" (on Windows) or a ".pkg" extension (on a Mac) and might be called something like "python-3.8.2.exe."

5. Once the package is downloaded, double-click it to run the Python installer.

6. You'll need to give the application permission to make changes to your device. This might require an administrator's password. Ask a parent, teacher, or guardian if you're not sure what it is.

7. Select any folder on your computer to store your Python files. Often, it's easiest to use the default location (the one the computer selects).

8. You should get a "Setup was successful" message. Congratulations—you've successfully installed Python! Go ahead and close the installer.

All About File Extensions

Every piece of information on your computer, from pictures to videos to songs, is stored in your computer as a sequence of 0s and 1s. The **file extension** tells your computer how to interpret that sequence. Otherwise, the 1s and 0s are just gibberish!

You might be familiar with some of these file extensions that appear at the end of file names:

* Text documents: .doc, .docx, .txt, .rtf

* Images: .jpg, .gif, .png

* Songs: .mp3, .wav

* Videos: .mp4, .mov, .mpg

Programmers use even more funny file extensions. Once you start making programs in Python, you'll see that your Python code is stored in .py files. Other coding languages have their own file extensions, like .java or .c.

Files with .exe, .app, .bin, or .vb are called "executables." When you double-click on them, a program opens and starts running. Executables contain "machine code." Every program on your computer, from your image editor to your web browser to Python, is an executable.

Symbol Key: Unlocking the Secrets of Python Syntax

Programmers use lots of symbols in their code. Each symbol is used to give the program different instructions. Here are some of the most common symbols you'll use in Python:

( ) - round brackets   / - forward slash

[ ] - square brackets   \ - backslash

{ } - curly braces   > - greater-than symbol

; - semicolon   < - less-than symbol

: - colon

IDLE

The Python package you downloaded contains both translation software and a program called IDLE.

IDLE is an **IDE**. IDE stands for "integrated development environment," but don't worry about remembering that acronym! An IDE is just a program that helps you edit and run code.

As long as you have a translator installed on your computer, you could technically write your code in any program that lets you type words and symbols. There are several advantages to using an IDE, though. First, there are lots of cool features that make writing code easier. These include things like syntax highlighting, which uses different colors to make Python keywords stand out.

Most IDEs also come with features like code completion and auto-indentation. When you're learning to code, it's best to keep these features turned on. They're helpful tools that are great for beginners who are just starting out! Once you've gotten more advanced and you're working on bigger projects, it's nice to have these shortcuts to help code more quickly.

Second, running your code in an IDE is simple. Just click a button and your code is transformed into a program.

The terms IDE and IDLE look very similar—after all, they're only one letter apart! Just remember that IDLE is the name of one specific program, while an IDE is a type of program.

IDLE is a great choice for beginners because it is simple, has all the best IDE features (like syntax highlighting and auto-indenting), and is automatically installed when you download Python!

There are lots of different IDEs you can use to write and run Python. Some IDEs are made by nonprofit coding organizations and others are created by private companies. Some are free and some aren't. All of them have slightly different features. If you're interested, search for "Python IDEs" in a web search engine, and you'll find lots of people talking about the pros and cons of each choice.

Every IDE, however, has two important parts: the editor and the console.

The Console and Editor

The **code editor** (often just called the **editor**) is the window where you actually write your Python code. When you run your program, the translator takes this code and turns it into machine instructions. These instructions are then executed line by line, with the results displayed in the **console**. The console is a separate window used just to display a program's output.

Picture an IDE as a puppet show stage. The audience only sees the glamorous final production. This is like looking at the console! If you look behind the stage, however, you'll see the puppeteers hiding, as well as all the tools they're using to manipulate their puppets. This is like looking at the editor.

When you're writing code, you need to be the puppeteer pulling the strings, but you also want to experience the show as the audience. Having the editor and console in the same program makes it easy to switch between views.

So, if you create a program that draws a picture of a kitten, the picture will appear in the console. If you write a "choose your own adventure" game where you're the hero, the story itself is displayed in the console. The code to make everything work stays in the editor.

Using IDLE

If you're on a Mac, click on your Launchpad. If you're on Windows, click the "Windows" button at the bottom of your screen. Then, for both operating systems, you can search for "IDLE" and click on the program to launch it. Or you can scroll around until you see the Python logo and access the IDLE shell from there.

A small white window will appear on your screen. This is your IDLE shell.

Picture the shell as a cross between an editor and a console. For starters, you can write lines of code directly into the shell. As soon as you hit "enter," the code runs immediately! The results are then displayed in the shell, right underneath your code:

```
Python 3.7.4 Shell
Python 3.7.4 (v3.7.4:e09359112e, Jul  8
2020, 14:54:52)
[Clang 6.0 (clang-600.0.57)] on darwin
Type "help", "copyright", "credits" or "
license()" for more information.
>>> 5 + 3
8
>>> print("Hi!")
Hi!
>>> 4 * 4
16
>>>



                                    Ln: 5  Col: 0
```

In this picture, you can see the shell with some Python code already written. The results of each line of code appear in blue. Don't worry if the code doesn't make sense yet—that's what the rest of this book is for! You can try it out now or wait until the next chapter.

This shell is different from the traditional editor/console setup, where code and results are separate. In the traditional editor, you can write many lines of code before trying them out. In the shell, it's always one line at a time.

There are pros and cons to using the shell. On the plus side, it's great for trying out new code! You instantly see the result of each line, so you know exactly what the code is doing and where any errors are. When following the examples in this book, it's easiest to write your code in the shell.

If you want to write long, complicated programs, it's better to write in a traditional code editor. Luckily, IDLE has an option for this as well, which we'll explore in the next section. Use this traditional code editor when you're coding chapter activities or examples that have many lines of code.

Using a Code Editor

Writing in a traditional editor allows you to edit and save your work. You can write some code, take a break, and come back to it later!

At the top of the shell screen, click "File" and then "New File." You should see a whole new window pop up. This blank file is your code editor. The original shell will serve as your console.

For easy viewing, you can set up the windows side by side, with the editor on the left and the console/shell on the right:

```
untitled
```

```
Python 3.7.4 (v3.7.4:e09359112e, Jul
 8 2020, 14:54:52)
[Clang 6.0 (clang-600.0.57)] on darw
in
Type "help", "copyright", "credits"
or "license()" for more information.
>>> 5 + 3
8
>>> print("Hi!")
Hi!
>>> 4 * 4
16
>>>
```

Ln: 1 Col: 0   Ln: 10 Col: 4

The console/shell still has the example code from earlier. The editor is blank—no new code has been written yet.

Another option is to make both the editor and the console full-screen, and switch back and forth between them. Whatever you prefer!

HACKER HINTS:
LIGHT VS DARK MODE

In IDLE, you can customize the color of your background and your text!

"Light mode" has a white background with dark text, and "night mode" or "dark mode" is a dark background with light text. Many programmers prefer night/dark mode because they find it less tiring on their eyes.

To change your settings on a Mac, click on "IDLE," then "Preferences," then "Highlights." On Windows, go to the "Options" in your shell, then "Configure IDLE," then "Highlights."

Saving Your Work

When working in the editor, you will need to save your work before you run your code—plus, you don't want your hard work to disappear!

To save your code file, click "File" and then "Save." In the editor, a small dialogue box will appear. Pick a name for your file and then save it anywhere you like. Pick a folder that's easy to remember (the default location always works).

Double-check that your file is being saved as a ".py" file. This will let the translator know that it's a Python file, not an image, text, video, or a different programming language. Otherwise, the Python keywords won't be highlighted correctly.

To load a file, click "File" and then "Open," and find your file's location. You may also see your program under "Recent Files."

Running a Program

Your editor is open, your code is written, and your file is saved. Now it's time to see if your program works as planned!

"Running" a program means translating it into machine code, then getting your computer to follow your code's instructions line by line. So, if you wrote a program where a tiny 2D sprite goes on adventures, then it's time for the computer to animate that 2D sprite going on adventures! If you wrote a program that writes your name in giant bold letters, it's time for the computer to create those letters, pixel by pixel.

To run your code, click the "Run" button in the top banner on your screen and then "Run Module." You'll see the results displayed in the console:

```
test1.py - /Users/pjfos/Documents/test1.py (3.7.4)
print(5 * 3)
print("Hi!")
print(4 * 4)




                                          Ln: 4   Col: 0
```

```
●  ●  ●            Python 3.7.4 Shell
>>>
================== RESTART: /Users/p
jfos/Documents/test1.py ============
======
15
Hi!
16
>>>
>>>
>>> |
>>>
>>>
>>>
>>>
>>>
>>>
>>>
>>>
                                          Ln: 17  Col: 4
```

In this picture, there's now some code in the editor! The file was saved as "test1.py" (you can see the name in the title bar). The result of the code is then displayed in blue in the console/shell. See how the code is now completely separate from the result?

One of the great things about using an editor is that you can run a program as many times as you want. There's no cost if you mess up! You're not using up art supplies, building materials, or sports equipment. If things don't go as planned, you can stop your program, fix a few lines, and try again—all in seconds!

Bugs

Even the best programmers get bugs. It doesn't matter how much you study or practice—it's just about impossible to write perfect code all the time.

There are two ways to know that your program has a bug. First, the program might "crash." It'll look something like this:

```
test1.py - /Users/pjfos/Documents/test1.py (3.7.4)
print(5 * 3)
print("Hi!")
print(4 * 4)
print(test1)



                                                    Ln: 5   Col: 0
```

```
                                    Python 3.7.4 Shell
>>>
>>>
================= RESTART: /Users/p
jfos/Documents/test1.py ============
======
15
Hi!
16
Traceback (most recent call last):
  File "/Users/pjfos/Documents/test1
.py", line 4, in <module>
    print(test1)
NameError: name 'test1' is not defin
ed
>>>
>>>
>>>
>>>
                                    Ln: 46   Col: 4
```

Errors in your console can look very dramatic with all that red text! Instead of trying to understand what everything means, focus on the *line number* that caused the crash. This will always be shown somewhere in your error message. In this picture, for example, it says "line 4." Often, this line of code has a small typo that you need to fix. Other times, the typo is actually higher up and it just took a few lines before the mistake caused the crash.

The second type of bug is less dramatic, but it's still a problem. Your code doesn't crash, but it's not giving you the results you expected.

We call these "logic errors." After you've written your program, it's a good idea to test it with different kinds of input to see if the program does what you expect. If you've built a pet simulator, for example, you'll want to test eating, sleeping, and playing with toys. If your cat is hungrier after eating, something wonky is going on!

There's an entire section at the end of this book called Bug Hunting: Troubleshooting Tips (see page 176). If you run into trouble, check it out. But don't worry about bugs too much. As you master your coding tools, you'll also learn about common mistakes and what to look for when your code doesn't work. Instead of getting discouraged, think of bugs as challenges! Coding is all about trial and error, and making mistakes is how we learn. You might even find yourself having fun while debugging!

(see page 176)

HACKER HINTS:
KEYBOARD SHORTCUTS

You may be familiar with the shortcuts "CTRL + C" and "CTRL + V" to copy and paste text (or "CMD + C" and "CMD + V" on a Mac). Just like these shortcuts, every IDE has different shortcuts for copying text, running programs, and saving your work. It's a good idea to go online and learn the keyboard shortcuts when you're using IDLE or a new IDE. It'll save you time in the long run!

3

Variables

Like we learned in chapter 1, **variables** are tools that help us keep track of changing information. Picture them as containers. The container itself isn't super important. It's the stuff inside that matters!

Have you ever helped organize a birthday party? To make everything run smoothly, you need to know who's invited, what activities are planned, and what kind of cake you're serving. But what if the information keeps changing? One minute you have seven guests, and the next you have fifteen. Suddenly, you need a bigger cake.

If you use variables to store your plans, it's easy to keep information organized and up-to-date.

The Basics of Variables

There are two parts to every variable: a name and a value, which can be changed anytime. In Python, you declare a variable like this:

```
cake = "chocolate"
```

Go ahead and type the code into IDLE shell, your IDLE editor, or whatever IDE you're using. The best way to learn to code is by trying things out!

To keep your program organized, the names of your variables should be clues about what information they store. Write the variable name on the left-hand side of your statement—in this case, it's "cake." On the right, you'll put the data, known as the value. In this case, it's "chocolate." And in the middle, we have the "=" sign, also known as the **assignment operator**.

The assignment operator assigns the value "chocolate" to the variable "cake." So if you wrote:

```
"chocolate" = cake
```

You'd be trying to assign the variable "cake" to the value "chocolate," and your code won't work!

What if you decide that chocolate isn't your favorite flavor of cake? To change the value of the "cake" variable, add a second line in your editor:

```
cake = "chocolate"
```

```
cake = "buttercream"
```

The first line slips the value "chocolate" into the variable "cake." The second line throws out the original value and replaces it with "buttercream." Because we use the same variable name (it's still about cake), we don't create a new variable. Same container, new content!

Print Function: Your First Code!

Ready to flex your coding muscles? The *print* function is a tool used to send messages to users. You're not printing on paper, though. **Printing** is computer-speak for displaying text in the console.

The most basic version looks like this:

```
print()
```

Then, we place the message we want to share inside the round brackets.

Traditionally, programmers start by printing "Hello World." But since every programmer does this, Earth's probably getting a little tired of that greeting.

In your code editor, let's write:

```
print("Hello Mars!")
```

Run your code to see your message displayed in the console. If you're using the IDLE editor, and you want to review how to run code, flip back to chapter 2 (page 11) for a quick refresher!

Congratulations—you've just written your first program!

If you get an error message, don't worry! Double-check your spelling for things like apostrophes and brackets, then try again.

Here are some general rules for writing code and using the *print* function:

- Every open bracket (round or square) *must* be closed by a matching bracket.

- Watch out for spelling mistakes in your message!

- The *print* function displays the exact text we've written, including uppercase and lowercase letters, spaces, and punctuation.

- The text inside the *print* function should always be surrounded by quotation marks.

Next, let's try printing some variables:

```
planet = "Jupiter"

print(planet)
```

If you run this code, you'll see "Jupiter" appear in the console. When you print a variable, you display its *value*, not its name. A variable's name just helps you—the programmer—keep track of your data. Your users never see it!

If we want to print a variable's value (in this case, "Jupiter") *and* text (in this case, "Hello") together in one message, we need to get a little fancy, and use an **f-string**. An f-string is a string that includes text *and* variables.

First create a variable:

```python
planet = "Jupiter"
```

Next, write out the print statement. Add the letter "f" in front of the text to indicate that it's an f-string. To include a variable, simply surround the variable's name with curly braces. Python will swap in the variable's value automatically:

```python
print(f"Hello {planet}!")
```

The result of your *print* function should be "Hello Jupiter!"

Using variables makes it easy to change values, which is useful when you don't want your messages to all be the same. Just remember, whenever you print a message with a variable, you need to use an f-string!

Types of Variables

There are two basic types of information we store in variables: text (like letters and words) and numbers.

Technically, both text and code are written with words and letters. But in coding, "text" means values stored inside variables or messages displayed to the user. "Code" is everything the user *doesn't* see, including variable names, math equations, and keywords like "print."

To let Python know we're writing text, we need to surround those words with quotation marks. For example:

```python
party_theme = "Pirates vs Ninjas"

first_game = 'Foam Noodle Sword Fight'
```

As you can see in the code above, it doesn't matter if you use single or double quotes!

Numbers, on the other hand, don't need any special syntax. See how the following numbers don't have any quotation marks around them:

```
num_party_hats = 20

num_prizes = 5
```

In these variable names, "num" is short for "number." So "`num_party_hats`" is used to store the number of available party hats. Much easier to read and write! We'll talk about how to choose good variable names in the next section.

Variable Dos and Don'ts!

Here are some dos and don'ts when creating and using variables:

- Be specific when naming variables. Descriptive names help us remember what our variables store.

- Always start your variable's name with a letter. After the first letter, you can use a mix of numbers and letters. Don't use spaces or special symbols like !, *, $, etc.

HACKER HINTS:
CHOOSING GOOD NAMES FOR YOUR VARIABLES

If your variable names are too similar, you might accidentally use the wrong one in a calculation. Imagine coding (or playing) a soccer game where scoring goals gives points to the other team instead! You can avoid this by giving your variables long but specific names, like score_team_red and score_team_blue.

- Capitalization matters! Uppercase "Cake" and lowercase "cake" are two different variables. In general, you should only use lowercase letters.

- Some keywords are reserved for coding instructions, like "and," "or," "list," "print," "for," and "while." These keywords will be highlighted in your IDE, so you'll know when you try to use something off-limits!

- If a variable name has multiple words, they should be separated by underscores, like "treasure_hunt_prize."

Calculating with Variables

We can use variables to make a lot of things easier, like calculating sums of numbers. For example, when you write out equations in math class, you might write something like this:

```
250 / 10 = 25
```

This is great for math, but not so great for programming. For starters, math is the *machine's* job!

Instead of crunching the numbers yourself, let the computer do it, then store the result in a variable.

```
n = 250 / 10
```

If you run this code, the value "25" will be calculated and then stored inside the variable "n."

Any variable storing a number can be used inside a math equation. Let's say you buy a giant container with 250 jelly beans and you want to split it equally between 10 party guests. You might declare the following variables:

```
num_guests = 10

num_jelly_beans = 250
```

Now, to calculate how many jelly beans go in each party bag:

```
jelly_beans_per_bag = num_jelly_beans / num_guests
```

Using variables might seem like an extra step, but there are lots of advantages to coding this way:

1. By naming them "num_jelly_beans" and "num_guests," it's clear what the values "250" and "10" represent. If you come back to your code a year from now, it's easier to remember what you were trying to calculate.

2. If you invite more guests to the party or buy another container of jelly beans, you can easily update your values.

3. Storing the result allows you to reuse it in your code. Maybe someday, you'll want to calculate the number of objects in each party bag. This is easy to do with your current code!

Using Operators

There are lots of different calculations we can do with variables. All basic math operators have a Python equivalent or symbol:

- Addition: +
- Subtraction: -
- Multiplication: *
- Division: /
- Exponentiation: **

Since the variable's name always goes on the left, your math goes on the right. Now that we've seen how to use basic math operators in Python, let's learn how they work together.

Order of Operations

Look at the following math problem:

```
n = 3 + 2 * 4
```

When you have an expression with multiple variables like this, how do you know which numbers are calculated first? The 3 + 2? Or the 2 * 4? Well, the acronym "BEDMAS" can help us figure this out. You might already be familiar with this concept from math class!

- **B** - brackets
- **E** - exponents
- **D** - division
- **M** - multiplication
- **A** - addition
- **S** - subtraction

Take another look at this equation:

```
n = 3 + 2 * 4
```

Will the value of "n" be 20 or 11?

If you guessed "11," you're correct! Multiplication (M) comes before addition (A) in BEDMAS!

But if we change it to:

```
n = (3 + 2) * 4
```

Now the result is "20," because brackets (B) are evaluated first.

If the same operator is used multiple times, then the order of operations goes from left to right—the same way you read!

Variables in Action

Now that you know all about variables, let's see what kind of programs you can build with this new tool! If you've been working in the shell up until now, this is a great time to try using a separate editor. It'll be much easier to tweak and edit your code.

Walkie-Talkie Codes

Imagine you're a secret agent on a mission in the tropical jungle! There are no cell towers here, so you and your team have to use walkie-talkies to communicate undercover.

Start by picking your super-secret codename and storing it inside a variable. Here, we've used "Eagle One"—what will you choose?

```
codename = "Eagle One"
```

Feel free to choose something goofy or exciting! If you're looking for ideas, try starting with a cool animal. Add your lucky number and you've got a great codename.

Next, use the *print* function to send a message to your team:

```
print(f"Go for {codename}. Over!")
```

Since your message contains a variable (your codename), you need to use an f-string. Remember to put the "f" outside of the quotation marks.

Run your code to see the result in the console. Now that your team knows you're ready for action, they can send you a response.

Let's create a new variable to store the codename for home base:

```
home_base = "Purple Viper"
```

And finally, add a return message:

```
print(f"Copy that, {codename}. This is {home_base}. We've
established contact with the satellite. Over!")
```

If you ever want to use a different codename, it's easy to update your variable to try new ones.

CODE COMPLETE!

```
codename = "Eagle One"

print(f"Go for {codename}. Over!")

home_base = "Purple Viper"

print(f"Copy that, {codename}. This is {home_base}. We've
established contact with the satellite. Over!")
```

YOUR TURN!

Congratulations—you've completed your first activity! Now that you've worked with variables, print statements, and f-strings, challenge yourself to make these changes to the code:

☐ Add one or two more teammates, each with their own codename and variable.

☐ Maybe one of your teammates turns traitor! Update their codename in your program. Remember, you don't have to create a new variable to do this; just put a new value into the old variable.

☐ Using *print* functions, send each other a few more messages to complete the mission. Remember, you only need to use f-strings if a message contains variables. And when you're done, don't forget to say "Over and out!"

Alien Socks

LEVEL UP!

A group of eight Martians are visiting Earth on vacation, but they all forgot to pack socks! Sadly, Earth socks are sold in pairs, and Martians have 17 legs each. The Martians are asking for our help to figure how many pairs of socks they need and how much they will cost.

We *could* calculate this by hand, but since we're practicing coding, let's see how variables can help! To start, let's set up a few numeric variables:

```
num_martians = 8

martian_legs = 17
```

Next, let's figure out how many socks the whole group of Martians needs. We can do this with a simple multiplication equation, and store the result in a new variable:

```
num_socks = num_martians * martian_legs
```

This is the total *number* of socks, but as you know, Earth socks are sold in pairs! So we'll want to divide the result by two. Update the line of code in your editor:

```
num_socks = num_martians * martian_legs / 2
```

The next step is to figure out the total price of this sock purchase. Let's start by storing the price of a single pair of socks:

```
sock_price = 1.25
```

Next, we'll multiply the price of this single pair of socks by the number of pairs needed:

```
total_sock_price = sock_price * num_socks
```

Finally, let's print the result to the console so our alien friends can see!

```
print(total_sock_price)
```

Did you get $85 for an answer?
That's a lot of money for socks—aren't you glad *you* don't have 17 legs?

CODE COMPLETE!

```
num_martians = 8

martian_legs = 17

num_socks = num_martians * martian_legs / 2
```

```
sock_price = 1.25

total_sock_price = sock_price * num_socks

print(total_sock_price)
```

YOUR TURN!

You just wrote a program with numeric variables *and* made some intergalactic friends! Here are some ideas to challenge yourself further and make your program even better:

☐ What if more aliens arrive, this time from Neptune? These aliens have six legs and forgot their socks, too. How can you change your code to work for this new species? Should you define new variables or update old ones?

☐ Let's say our alien friends want to stay on Earth for nine days and they want clean socks for each new day. How can you add this into your equation?

A Likely Story!

Ready to get creative and build your own interactive story? To begin, you'll write a short story or joke with a few words replaced by variables. For now, don't worry about the value of these variables. We'll fill them in later!

Here's an example to get you started. You can copy it into your editor or write your own story instead. Because our story contains variables, we'll use f-strings, so don't forget the "f" symbol in front of the quotation marks.

```
print(f"Once upon a time, {name} went to the zoo. But a
{adjective} {animal} escaped and chased them around!")
```

Now we'll create our missing variables. Normally, we give variables their values when we declare them, like this:

```
name = "Sophie"
```

But this time, we're doing something a little different. Instead of picking values ourselves, we're letting our user choose!

The **input** function allows you to have a conversation with your user. This function does two things. First, it asks the user a question or gives a direction, which is printed to the console. The user can then type their response in the console—right next to the question or direction—and hit the Enter key. Second, the *input* function copies the user's answer and stores it in a variable.

A basic *input* function looks like this:

```
name = input()
```

Just like the *print* function, the *input* function uses rounded brackets. Usually, you include a **text prompt** inside these brackets. A text prompt is a sentence that tells the user what they need to do. That prompt is printed on the screen and tells the user what kind of value they need to enter.

Since the *input* function displays our message letter for letter, it's a good idea to include a space after the colon. That way your message won't look smushed together and will make sense for the user.

```
name = input("Enter a name: ")
```

Like all statements with variables, the variable's name goes on the left, the "=" symbol in the middle, and the value on the right. In this case, the value is chosen by the user after seeing the text prompt and stored in our "name" variable.

To finish off your code, declare any other variables missing from your story. In the example, we're still missing the "animal" and "adjective" variables:

```
animal = input("Enter an animal: ")
```

```
adjective = input("Enter an adjective: ")
```

Quick tip: The lines of code declaring your variables should be placed at the beginning of your program. Otherwise, Python won't be able to run the print statement, because your variables don't contain any values yet!

Congratulations! You've just created an interactive text game that you can play with friends, family, or even by yourself!

CODE COMPLETE!

```python
name = input("Enter a name: ")

animal = input("Enter an animal: ")

adjective = input("Enter an adjective: ")

print(f"Once upon a time, {name} went to the zoo. But a
{adjective} {animal} escaped and chased them around!")
```

YOUR TURN!

The best way to improve your programming skills is to practice! Now that you've coded this activity, see if you can make the following changes to your code:

☐ If you copied the example story, try writing your own! Don't be afraid to put your characters in ridiculous situations. How long can you make *your* story?

☐ Add a few more variables to your story. Maybe this means adding more text, maybe not. What are some good prompts for your users?

☐ What do you think is better for your story: one long print statement or multiple shorter print statements? Try out both and see what you prefer!

Variables Off-Screen

Just like there are variables in programming, you've probably run into variables off-screen, in the real world!

If your parents say, "We're going to the beach Saturday!", you can guess that the outing will involve swimsuits, snacks, and beach games. But which ones?

Usually, you wait until the last minute to decide on the actual details. You might wake up and choose your polka-dot swimsuit instead of your orange one. Right before leaving, you pack popsicles instead of ice cream sandwiches.

Making these tiny choices in advance isn't always useful. Maybe you chose the orange swimsuit, but it's in the laundry, so you're stuck with the polka-dot one. The world is impossible to predict!

Making plans with vague, general ideas is like using variables. You can figure out the values at "runtime." Now you're thinking like a programmer!

HACKER HINTS:
HARD CODING

Maybe you're calculating how many hours you sleep in a year, and you use the number "365" instead of creating a new variable called "days_in_a_year." Using the value directly (in this case, 365) instead of storing it in a variable is called "hard coding." And the code works fine—until suddenly it's a leap year! Now you have to dig through all your code to update the values. What a pain!

To simplify your life, use as many variables as you can. You never know when information needs to be changed.

Coder's Checklist

In this chapter, we covered:

- ☐ How to declare variables

- ☐ The two kinds of information you store in variables: text and numbers

- ☐ How to write a simple *print* function and use an f-string to format text

- ☐ How to do math with variables, and how to use the order of operations (BEDMAS)

If anything in this list feels unfamiliar or confusing, you can always flip back through the chapter. Coding is a skill that takes practice—just like baseball, guitar, or handstands. The best way to learn is by typing code in your editor, running your program, and seeing what happens—over and over again!

4

Data Types

Data comes in all shapes and sizes. There are big numbers, small numbers, decimal numbers, as well as text values and values that can only be "yes" or "no." The "type" of your value determines how the computer stores it in memory. Each data type also responds differently to math operators like +, -, *, and /.

Think of data types like different animals! A horse needs a big stable, but a cat just needs a cozy bed. A dog enjoys playing in water, while a cat will hiss and run away if it gets wet. Each animal has different needs and different behaviors.

Python automatically knows how to store each data type, but it's important for us, the programmers, to understand how to work with them!

Strings

String is the computer term for text. It comes from the idea of "stringing" together letters to make words, sentences, and pages.

To tell Python that a value is a string, we surround it with either single or double quotes, like this:

```
favorite_animal = "squid"
```

This is something you've seen already in this book, right? But what if we write:

```
num_tentacles = "2"
```

What happens now? Because we used quotation marks, the "number" 2 will be stored as the "letter" 2. Python treats it like text! Numbers can become strings, same as letters and words.

So, if you write the following code in your editor:

```
num_limbs = 6 + num_tentacles
```

Python doesn't know how to add numbers and strings together, so you'll get an error when you run your code. You're adding a number with words, and that doesn't make sense!

So why would we ever store numbers as strings? Well, for starters, not all numbers are meant to be added, multiplied, or crunched inside an equation. Telephone numbers and zip codes are both great examples. For instance, you'd never write code like this:

```
alice_telephone = 4161112222

bob_telephone = 4163334444

super_mega_telephone = alice_telephone + bob_telephone
```

Other times, you'll want your variable to act like a string, so you can glue it together with another string using the + operator, or repeat it using the * operator.

Adding Values in Strings

We can't add strings to numbers, but we *can* add strings to other strings. This isn't like adding numbers, where 1 + 1 = 2 and 2 + 2 = 4. When you add strings, you're gluing blocks of text together.

Try out the following code to see what adding strings together looks like:

```
pet_name = "Thomas"

pet_type = "turtle"

pet = pet_name + " the " + pet_type

print(pet)
```

When you run this code, you should see "Thomas the turtle" in your console.

Multiplying Values in Strings

We can't add numbers and strings, but we can *multiply* strings by numbers! What do you think will happen when we multiply the string "Thomas" by 5? Let's experiment!

```
pet_name = "Thomas"

print(pet_name * 5)
```

If you guessed "ThomasThomasThomasThomasThomas," you're correct! Multiplying a string by a number (in this case, 5) creates a new, super long string where the original string is glued together five times. This is useful if you're creating text games, where letters and numbers are used to create maps and images. For example, you might make a maze where the walls are made of Xs.

Just so you know, while you can add two strings together or multiply a string by a number, you can't multiply two strings together or divide two strings.

Numbers

Numbers are the next type of data type. In computer science, there are two species of numbers. **Integers** (ints) are whole numbers, like 7, 0, or 20,000. **Floating point numbers** (floats) are decimal numbers like 3.14 or 0.5.

To a computer, the difference is huge. The way a computer stores ints versus floats in its memory is as different as a fish tank is from a birdcage. Luckily, Python detects data types automatically, so we humans don't have to worry about it!

Can you mix ints and floats in an equation? You bet! Give this a try:

```
print(2 + 4.2)
```

You should see "6.2" in the console. Python automatically did the conversion between floats and ints!

Integer Division

When you divide two integers, you often end up with a floating point number. Sometimes, though, you don't want a pesky decimal! In that case, you can use integer division.

Check out the following code:

```
num_treats = 10

num_puppies = 3

print(num_treats / num_puppies)

print(num_treats // num_puppies)
```

The first print statement displays the number 3.333333333333335. The second displays a simple 3. The only difference between the two lines is the single backslash versus double backslash when dividing. We refer to the double backslash as integer division.

If you try to divide 10 treats between 3 puppies, math will tell you that each puppy should get 3.333333333333335 treats. But sometimes, fractions aren't practical. Maybe you want to save that remaining treat for later or the treat is too small to split.

The solution is to use integer division. This operator will always round down your answer into a nice whole number that's easier to work with.

Floats

Decimal numbers can go on forever. No matter how precise your fraction is, you can always stick one more number onto the end!

At some point, though, this becomes ridiculous. Getting an extra half of a pie is awesome. An extra quarter is great. An extra 1/100 is a little silly. And an extra 1/100,000,000 probably isn't even a crumb!

In Python, floats are limited to 16 digits. At some point, programmers decided this was the sweet spot between accuracy and too much storage. Unless you're doing science or finance, it's unlikely you'll even need *that* much precision!

Integers to Strings: Converting Between Data Types

What if we need to change one data type into another? We can turn an int into a string with the *str* function:

```
a = str(2)
```

In this example, the *str* function takes the number 2 and converts it into the string 2. Then, it stores the result in the variable "a." We can treat "a" like a string! For example, we could multiply it by 10 and print the result:

```
print(a * 10)
```

You should see "2222222222" in your console. That wouldn't happen if "a" was storing the number 2–you'd get 20. In this case, since you were multiplying a string by a number, you got that string duplicated–just like when you got ThomasThomasThomasThomasThomas on page 41!

We can also turn strings into integers with the *int* function.

```
b = int("2")
```

Here, the *int* function takes the string 2 and turns it into the number 2, which it stores in the variable "b." The *int* function can only convert strings that are built out of numbers. If you put something weird between the round brackets, like a letter or a symbol, you'll get an error.

Boolean Types

Another type of data are **Booleans**, which can only have two values: True or False. Usually, you use Booleans for variables that are answers to yes/no questions. Did the user win the game? Did they enter their password correctly?

We often start the name of a Boolean variable with the word "is." This makes it really clear that the value stored inside should either be True or False.

```
is_puppy_cute = True

is_cat_hungry = False
```

Like all variables, you can change these values at any time.

In Python, "True" and "False" are special keywords used for Booleans. Since they are keywords, make sure you capitalize that first letter, or you'll get an error message! Also, True and False are Booleans, *not* strings, so you don't need to surround them with quotation marks.

Comparing Values

We've already seen mathematical operators like +, -, *, and /. These operators take two or more values (like 5 and 7) and use math to combine them to make a new value (like 12 or 35).

There are also comparison operators.

The most common is the **equals-to operator** (==), which tells you if two values are equal. For example:

```
5 == 7
```

Since 5 and 7 are different numbers, they obviously can't be equal! Let's see what happens if you print out this comparison. You can put the whole expression in between round brackets—no quotation marks needed!

```
print(5 == 7)
```

In your console, you should see "False!"

Comparisons *always* return Boolean values. After all, either 5 equals 7 or it doesn't—and that's it!

There's also the **not-equals-to operator** (!=), which tells you when values are *different*. Let's try it out:

```
print(5 != 7)
```

While it's *False* that 5 equals 7, it's *True* that 5 *doesn't* equal 7. The not-equals-to operator always gives the opposite result of equals-to operator.

Assigning vs Comparing

When doing math in the real world, we use the single "=" sign to compare two values. But this doesn't work in coding! The single "=" is already reserved for the assignment operator, which puts a value inside a variable. We've used it a lot so far in earlier chapters.

Take a look at these two slightly different lines of code:

```
a = 5

a == 5
```

In the first line, we're storing the value "5" inside the variable "a." In the second line, we're comparing the value inside "a" to the value "5." The result of this comparison can either be True or False.

Don't worry if you mix up these two operators at first! Even experienced programmers sometimes make that mistake. But whenever you get a typo in your code, it's a good idea to check all your comparisons.

None Type

The "None" type is the black hole of variables. It's not a number. It's not a string of text that says "None." It's just . . . nothing!

```
current_pet = None
```

Since "None" isn't a string, you don't need to surround the value with quotation marks. Your Python editor will also highlight the word in a different color to show that it's a special concept!

You might see "None" when you get error messages. It's also a useful placeholder value when you want to define a variable without giving it a value.

Data Types in Action

Ready to practice using data types? C'mon, let's try it out! There's no better way to master a coding tool than by building things with it. Open a new editor window and let's get coding.

Kitten Party

LEVEL UP!

The Internet loves kittens! With a little bit of imagination, let's create our own virtual kitten. We'll use "=" for whiskers, "^" for ears, and "." for the nose. Then, we can print a bunch of kittens to the screen! In this activity, we'll also practice multiplying strings with numbers and converting strings to ints.

To start, let's make our kitten using a string. Don't forget to surround the string with quotation marks!

```
kitten = "=^.^="
```

Next, using the *input* function, let's ask the user how many kittens they want to adopt. Remember to put a good text prompt in between the brackets of your function:

```
num_kittens = input("How many kittens would you like?")
```

Whether the user wants 1 or 100 kittens, their choice will be stored in our "num_kittens" variable. However, the *input* function always returns string values and we want an actual number. After all, we can't multiply two strings together.

To fix this, let's convert our variable's value into an int:

```
num_kittens = int(num_kittens)
```

In this line of code, we removed the string value from the "num_kittens" container. Then we transformed it into an int using the *int* function and put it back in the same container!

To finish off, let's print out a line of kittens for the user to enjoy:

```
print(kitten * num_kittens)
```

Our "kitten" variable contains the text art, while "num_kittens" is an integer. Remember what happens when a string is multiplied by an int?

CODE COMPLETE!

```python
kitten = "=^.^="

num_kittens = input("How many kittens would you like?")

num_kittens = int(num_kittens)

print(kitten * num_kittens)
```

Depending on how many kittens you wanted, you should see a line of 5, 10, or maybe even 1,000 kittens purring all over your console!

YOUR TURN!

Now that you've practiced using strings and integers, see if you can make the following changes to your program:

☐ Try creating some new text animals, like a fish, bird, or turtle! If your picture is several lines tall, how could you tweak your code to display it properly? Hint: You'll need multiple variables for a single picture.

☐ Instead of printing "n" kittens, get creative—try printing "n * n" to the screen!

- -

Lie Detector

LEVEL UP!

Have you ever played "Two Truths and a Lie?" You start by coming up with three statements, two that are true and one that's a lie. The other players then have to guess which is which! We'll use Booleans to help us check if the user guessed correctly.

Let's start by printing some instructions for our user:

```python
print("Can you guess which statement is a lie?")
```

Now it's time to print our statements to the console. You can either follow the example or pick your own truths and lies.

```
print("1: I really love spiders!")

print("2: I've been inside a volcano.")

print("3: I can do a headstand!")
```

Ideally, you want it to be tricky to guess which statement is the lie. "I went to the moon," for example, might be a little hard to believe!

Next, we record the user's guess using the *input* function:

```
guess = input("Which statement is the lie? Enter 1, 2, or 3: ")
```

The *input* function always returns strings. So our "guess" variable should store either the string "1," the string "2," or the string "3." Should we convert it into a number?

Programmers like to be efficient. Unless we're doing mathematical things with the value, like adding or dividing, it's easier to leave it as a string, so we'll do that.

To finish the program, record which statement is the lie. Whether your lie is statement 1, 2, or 3, you want to store this number as a string so it matches the user's input:

```
lie = "1"
```

Finally, let's see if the user guessed correctly:

```
print(guess == lie)
```

We're using the equals-to operator (==), which means the result can either be True or False. If the user's guess matches the value in our "lie" variable, then the Boolean statement will be True. If they're tricked by our clever lie, then it'll be False!

CODE COMPLETE!

```
print("Can you guess which statement is a lie?")

print("1: I really love spiders!")

print("2: I've been inside a volcano.")

print("3: I can do a headstand!")
```

```
guess = input("Which statement is the lie? Enter 1, 2, or 3: ")

lie = "1"

print(guess == lie)
```

Challenge friends and family members to your new game. Let's see how many of them you can trick!

YOUR TURN!

Now that you've coded this activity, challenge yourself to tweak this game and make it even more exciting:

☐ Add another lie to your code so you have two lies and two truths. Give your user another guess and see if they can detect both false statements! (Hint: You'll need to add another *input* function and another comparison.)

☐ We originally kept the user's guess (1, 2, or 3) as a string, but what happens if you change it into an int? Do you think this makes the code better or just messier?

- -

Bake Sale: Raise Some Dough!

 LEVEL UP!

You and two other friends have decided to hold a bake sale to fundraise for your trip to the zoo. The end goal is $250. Using integers, floats, and mathematical operators, let's figure out how many tasty treats you need to sell!

To start, let's pick some baked goods and decide how many portions you will each bake. You can copy the example or pick your own desserts:

```
chocolate_cupcakes = 24

shortbread_cookies = 36

apple_pie_slices = 20
```

In total, you need to make $250. So how do you decide what prices to charge for each baked good?

Variables are easy to change, so you might as well start with your best guess. If you don't get the answer you want, just tweak your variables and run your code again!

```
cupcake_price = 2.00

cookie_price = 1.00

pie_price = 2.50
```

Putting the "00" after the decimal point does two things. First, it makes it clear to other programmers that those values represent money. Second, it tells Python that we want these values to be floats.

Now, let's figure out how much money we can earn by selling all our baked goods:

```
max_money = (chocolate_cupcakes * cupcake_price) +
(shortbread_cookies * cookie_price) + (apple_pie_slices *
pie_price)

print(max_money)
```

If you're following the example, you should get $134. That's just over half of what you need. You could increase your prices or bake twice as many portions. The choice is yours!

There's one more thing to consider. You probably won't sell all your snacks, no matter how delicious they look and smell. If you're lucky, you might sell 90 percent. If you're unlucky, it could be much less.

Let's create a new variable to include the percentage of snacks likely to be actually sold:

```
p = 75
```

Again, just use your best guess!

We're now all set to calculate an accurate estimate. Since "p" is a percentage, let's divide it by 100 inside our equation:

```
probable_money = max_money * (p / 100)
```

Try typing "75 / 100" in your IDLE shell. You should get 0.75. Python is a smart language that can automatically switch between integers and floats. Most languages aren't that smart, though, so it's a good idea to test out divisions before using them in a long coding program.

Finish by printing your "probable_money" variable:

```
print(probable_money)
```

You now have everything you need to estimate how much money your bake sale will make—and whether or not you'll get that trip to the zoo!

CODE COMPLETE!

```
chocolate_cupcakes = 24

shortbread_cookies = 36

apple_pie_slices = 20


cupcake_price = 2.00

cookie_price = 1.00

pie_price = 2.50


max_money = (chocolate_cupcakes * cupcake_price) +
(shortbread_cookies * cookie_price) + (apple_pie_slices *
pie_price)

print(max_money)


p = 75

probable_money = max_money * (p / 100)

print(probable_money)
```

Keep fiddling with your numbers until you find the magic combination that gets you over the $250 mark!

YOUR TURN!

The best way to master a coding tool is to play around with a program and try adding new things. Now that you've successfully coded this activity, here are a few ideas to challenge yourself further:

☐ A couple of new friends bring new baked goods to the sale. Try adding them into your equation. How would the equation change if you add two friends? What about three?

☐ What if you decide to hold the sale over several days and create new batches of treats every day? What new variables should you add to your equation?

Data Types Off-Screen

Humans love separating things by type, including data. You can see this all over the world outside your computer. We have different types of music: rock, pop, hip-hop, classical. And we have different types of movies, books, comic books—you name it!

All of these "types" are categories created by humans. We can create new types at any time.

Generally, we create a "type" for a particular purpose. We created spoons to eat soups. We created knives to help us cut meat. We created forks for pasta and salads. Each "type" is designed for a particular task. Imagine trying to eat soup with a fork!

See if you can notice the next time you see different "data" types out in the real world!

HACKER HINTS:
PRINT YOUR VARIABLES!

There's a downside to Python detecting data types automatically. Unless you wrote the code yourself, you can't be 100 percent sure what type of value a variable is storing. When in doubt, print your variables to the console. This is a good habit anyway, to make sure that your code is doing exactly what you planned.

Coder's Checklist

In this chapter, you learned:

☐ The difference between data types like strings, integers, floats, Booleans, and the "None" type

☐ How to add strings together

☐ How to multiply strings with integers

☐ How to convert between strings and numbers

☐ How to use comparison operators like "==" and "!="

☐ The difference between the assignment operator (=) and the equals-to operator (==)

You can flip through this chapter anytime you want to review data types. The more you use this tool, the more natural it'll feel to work with integers, strings, floats, and Booleans.

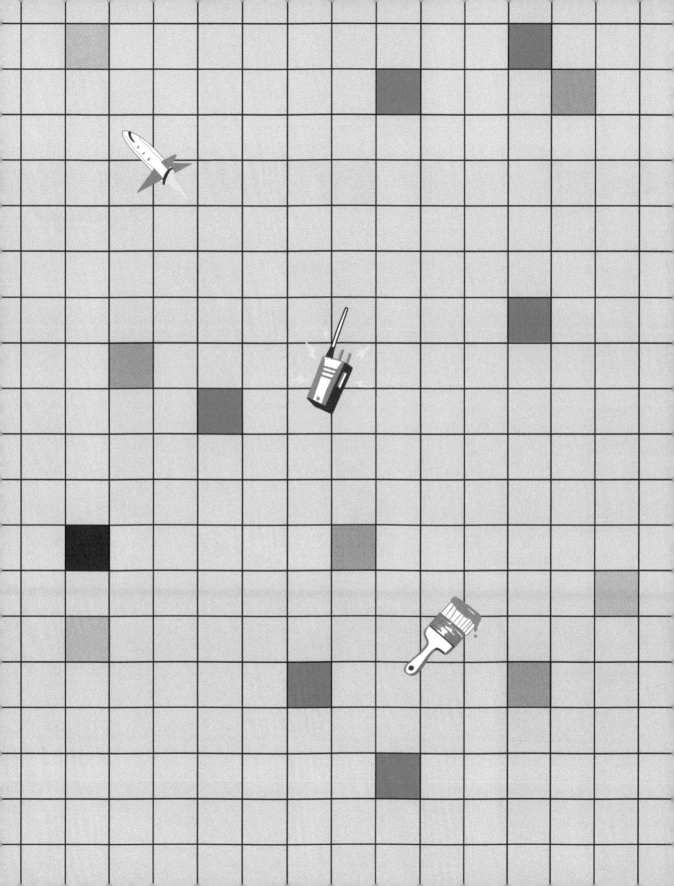

5

Data Structures

Data structures are tools that organize large amounts of data. When you've got millions (or billions!) of pieces of information, it doesn't make sense to put them all in separate variables. Imagine how long that code would be! Instead, data structures allow us to put a million pieces of data into a single mega-variable.

You can compare a data structure to a library full of books. The library uses an indexing system to quickly find any book you're looking for. New books can be added to the index and then placed onto the appropriate shelf. Much nicer than sifting through a giant, disorganized pile of books, right?

There are many different ways to index data and many types of data structures. Three of the most common are **lists**, **tuples**, and **dictionaries**.

Lists

Lists are a type of data structure with ordered items. Picture a row of books on a shelf or a line of ducklings.

Each book—or duckling, or string, or number—has a clear position. We know who's first and who's last. When talking about lists, we say "index" (or "indices") instead of "position."

In Python, we use square brackets to declare a list. Items are separated by commas. A list of numbers would look like this:

```
list_of_numbers = [5, 0, 7, 3, 3, 3, 1]
```

A list of strings would look like this:

```
list_of_animals = ["duck", "cat", "iguana", "duck", "parrot"]
```

The first item in "list_of_numbers" is "5," while the first item in "list_of_animals" is "duck." Did you notice the repeat items in each list? There are several 3s and two ducks. Because these items have different indices (positions), it's possible to tell the repeat items apart.

If you want to display your lists, you can print them to the console:

```
print(list_of_numbers)
```

```
print(list_of_animals)
```

But wait! You can also have lists of blended items:

```
blended_list = [5, "duck", 0, "horse", "emu", 7]
```

Declaring a list is similar to declaring any other variable. The name goes on the left, the "=" sign in the middle, and the data on the right. The only difference here is that we're storing a lot of data. And we're squashing it into a single container!

To search your list and grab a single item from the container, use the item's index:

```
list_of_animals[3]
```

Once again, you're using square brackets. This time, you'll start with the name of the variable storing your list, then put the value's index in square brackets. It's like looking at books on a shelf and telling the librarian that you want "the third book from the left."

Let's see what happens when we print out that third item!

```
print(list_of_animals[3])
```

The spelling looks a bit tricky here, because you've got square brackets inside round brackets. Make sure you close your inner pair before closing your outer pair!

When you run the code, you probably see the word "duck" in the console. Not what you were expecting, right?

In programming, lists begin at position 0—not position 1. So "duck" might be the first item in line, but it's at index 0, not index 1. "Cat" is then at index 1, and "iguana" is at index 2. So let's try modifying our print statement:

```
print(list_of_animals[2])
```

Now we've got an iguana in the console!

Starting at index 0 instead of index 1 feels a bit weird at first. Keep practicing and you'll master it in no time!

You can also change the value of any item in the list:

```
list_of_animals[2] = "snake"
```

"Snake" will now replace "iguana" at index 2, and iguana will disappear from the list.

Making Changes to Lists

To add new items to a list, we use the **append** function, like this:

```
list_of_animals.append("ferret")
```

To use "append":

- Start with your list variable (in this case, "list_of_animals").

- Next, put a period (.).

- Write "append," followed by round brackets.

- The round brackets will contain the item you're adding.

If you print out the whole list, you'll see the new value added on at the end. Try it out!

```
print(list_of_animals)
```

Any program can print text or read in text. But to add to a list, you need to have already created a list in a previous line.

That's why the syntax of *append* is a little different than functions like *print* or *input*. If you append to a variable that's not a list or a list that's not defined, you'll get an error.

To get rid of an item, use the *remove* function:

```
list_of_animals.remove("duck")

print(list_of_animals)
```

If there are two items with the same value, you'll only remove the first one. Of course, you can only remove items that are actually in the list—if you try to remove "rhino" from this list, you'll get an error message!

Finding the Smallest Number in a List

We've added and removed items from a list, but what about finding specific items?

To find the smallest number in a list, we use the *min* function (think of the word "minimum"). Let's define a list of numbers, try it out, and then print the result to the console:

```
list_of_numbers = [7, 5, 6]

smallest_val = min(list_of_numbers)

print(smallest_val)
```

In this code, *min* selected 5 as the smallest number. No surprise there!

By default, strings are ordered alphabetically in Python. So if you call *min* on a list of strings, you'll get the value that appears in the dictionary first.

```
list_of_sports = ["soccer", "baseball", "basketball",
"hockey"]

print(min(list_of_sports))
```

In this example, it's "baseball."

Now, both the *min* function and the *print* function have their own set of round brackets. So when we use them together, we get two closing brackets back to back. See how "min(list_of_sports)" fits inside "print()"? Just like a set of nesting dolls!

HACKER HINTS:
PRACTICE USING LISTS

If you're not comfortable working with lists yet, try writing out your list's items on paper. Over each item, jot down the index, starting at 0. This will help you see the difference between items (data) and indices (position). Eventually, you'll do this in your head automatically!

Slicing Lists

"Slicing" means separating a small chunk from a list. Think of it like slicing a cake so you don't need to eat the whole thing at once!

Let's start with a list of pets:

```
list_of_pets = ["cat", "dog", "guinea pig", "budgie",
"parrot", "iguana", "snake", "turtle"]
```

Let's say we only want the mammals. In that case, our slice should start at index 0 ("cat") and end at index 2 ("guinea pig"):

```
list_of_mammals = list_of_pets[0:3]
```

To code a list slice:

- Start with your list variable.

- Use square brackets.

- Inside the brackets, write your starting and ending index, separated by a colon.

- The ending index isn't included in your slice, so if you want your slice to include indices 0, 1, and 2, your ending index must be one higher (3).

So, slicing the list of birds would look like this:

```
list_of_birds = list_of_pets[3:5]
```

If you leave the starting index blank, Python assumes you want to start at the beginning of the list. And if you leave your ending index blank, Python assumes you want to go to the end. So, to get lists of mammals and reptiles, we could do the following:

```
list_of_mammals = list_of_pets[:3]

list_of_reptiles = list_of_pets[5:]
```

Unlike slicing a cake, slicing a list doesn't remove the items—it creates a copy! If you want to see this for yourself, try printing out all the lists, the original and the slices, in the same program.

Tuples

A **tuple** is a data structure that acts just like a list, with one key difference: Once the tuple has been created, its values can't be changed.

Creating a tuple is similar to creating a list, but you use round brackets instead of square brackets:

```
candies = ("gummy worms", "jawbreakers", "jujubes")
```

You can search and access individual items the same way as lists–with square brackets.

```
print(candies[0])
```

However, if you try to change an item, you'll get an error message. Try running the following code:

```
candies[0] = "lollipops"
```

There's also no way to add or remove elements. So why would a tuple be useful? Well, if you're working with a big team, using a tuple prevents other people from changing values and mixing things up (or keeps you from making that mistake yourself!). Tuples are also easier for computers to store in memory than regular lists.

Dictionaries

A **dictionary** is a collection of key-value pairs, just like a real dictionary, where each word is matched to its definition. Unlike the other data structures, which have a specific order with clear positions, data in a dictionary is all jumbled together.

Whenever you put a value into your dictionary, you link the value to a matching key term. The key is then used to fetch or update your value. Both keys and values can be any data type you want–integer, string, float! However, each key must be different so the dictionary knows what value it matches.

To declare a dictionary, we use curly braces instead of square brackets:

```
telephone_numbers = {"Josh": "444-111-0000"}
```

Here, we've created a dictionary with only one item and stored the whole data structure inside the variable "telephone_numbers." The number "444-111-0000" has been linked to the key "Josh." In each key-value pair, the key is written first, followed by a colon (:) and then the value.

To search the dictionary and access Josh's telephone number, we'd write:

```
telephone_numbers["Josh"]
```

Even though you declare a dictionary with curly braces, you still access items with square brackets—just like a list!

If Josh ever changes his telephone number, you can update it:

```
telephone_numbers["Josh"] = "444-111-1111"
```

Most of the time, we want more than one value in our dictionary. In Python, you declare a multi-valued dictionary like this:

```
telephone_numbers = {"Josh": "444-111-0000", "Kelly":
"750-200-2222", "Mariam": "762-816-3333"}
```

Each key is connected to its value with a colon. Then, each key-value pair is separated by a comma.

You can also start with an empty dictionary, like this:

```
telephone_numbers = {}
```

Then you can add your values one at a time:

```
telephone_numbers["Josh"] = "444-111-0000"

telephone_numbers["Kelly"] = "750-200-2222"

telephone_numbers["Mariam"] = "762-816-3333"
```

Dictionaries are great when you want to link two pieces of data: one that's important but complicated (like the phone numbers) and one that's easy to remember (like the names). Sometimes, indices just don't cut it!

Data Types in Action

Ready to create some fun programs with your new coding tool? Let's see what we can build with lists, tuples, and dictionaries!

- -

Pizza Pandemonium!

LEVEL UP!

The Pizza Pandemonium restaurant makes cheap, delicious pizza—but with super weird toppings. In fact, its orders are always random, so you never know what you're going to get! Using a list, let's cook up the strangest pizza you've ever tasted.

Start by creating a list of 10 different pizza toppings. Feel free to get creative and include weird things like anchovies, apples, or even macaroni and cheese! The stranger your ingredients, the more fun and bizarre the pizzas will be.

```
pizza_toppings = ["onion", "frogs' legs", "olives",
"pepperoni", "French fries", "pepper", "squid", "mushrooms",
"jalapeno", "pear"]
```

Next, pick three random numbers between 0 and 9. These will be the indices of the ingredients on your pizza. No peeking! Remember, we're choosing between 0 and 9 because lists start at index 0. So, if there are 10 items in the list, our last index is 9!

Let's store your choices in some variables:

```
t1 = pizza_toppings[3]

t2 = pizza_toppings[6]

t3 = pizza_toppings[7]
```

The "t" in our variable names stands for "topping."

Now, let's use an f-string to print out whatever extraordinary pizza we've concocted:

```python
print(f"Here is a {t1}, {t2}, and {t3} pizza!")
```

Think you could actually eat that pizza?

CODE COMPLETE!

```python
pizza_toppings = ["onion", "frogs' legs", "olives",
"pepperoni", "French fries", "pepper", "squid", "mushrooms",
"jalapeno", "pear"]

t1 = pizza_toppings[3]

t2 = pizza_toppings[6]

t3 = pizza_toppings[7]


print(f"Here is a {t1}, {t2}, and {t3} pizza!")
```

Run the program a few times and play around with different indices. Or ask your friends and family to pick the numbers for you. Let's see what bizarre creations you can dream up!

YOUR TURN!

Now that you've coded this activity, you can keep practicing coding with lists. Try making the following changes to your program:

☐ To increase your odds of making a delicious pizza, use the *remove* function to take away your least-favorite topping.

☐ Do we really need the "t1," "t2," and "t3" variables? Why or why not? How could you write the program without them?

My Friend, Chatbot

A "chatbot" is a program you can talk to via text. A sophisticated chatbot is hard to write, but we can create a simple one using a dictionary! Let's design a chatbot that can tell us about its favorite things.

To start, let's create an empty dictionary:

```
chatbot = {}
```

Next, let's add some key-value pairs. Each "key" will be a category, like food, color, animal, or planet. The "value" is the chatbot's favorite item in that category. For example, its favorite food might be tacos, or its favorite animal might be the platypus.

Since both the keys and values are strings, we can add a pair to the dictionary like this:

```
chatbot["animal"] = "platypus"
```

Let's add a few more pairs!

```
chatbot["color"] = "orange"
```

```
chatbot["food"] = "tacos"
```

```
chatbot["planet"] = "Mars"
```

You can add favorite things for as many categories as you want: numbers, movies, music, seasons. Once you're happy with your chatbot, it's time to make it interact with the user!

First, let's print out some instructions for talking to your chatbot:

```
print("Hi, I'm Chatbot! Ask me about my favorite animal,
color, food, or planet.")
```

Next, let's use the *input* function to copy the user's question into a variable:

```
key = input("What is Chatbot's favorite... ")
```

It's always a good idea to write a clear prompt. That way, the user knows that the program expects them to type something.

The "key" variable will store the string entered by the user. We're expecting this to be a single word, like "animal" or "food." Using this key, let's access the matching value in the dictionary. We'll store that value, or "val," in a new variable:

```
val = chatbot[key]
```

Now, let's print Chatbot's response to the console. To make it feel like a conversation, let's use an f-string:

```
print(f"My favorite {key} is {val}!")
```

If the user asked about Chatbot's favorite color, the string "color" would be stored in "key," and the string "orange" would be stored in "val." So Chatbot's response would be: "My favorite color is orange!"

5 CODE COMPLETE!

```
chatbot = {}

chatbot["animal"] = "platypus"

chatbot["color"] = "orange"

chatbot["food"] = "tacos"

chatbot["planet"] = "Mars"


print("Hi, I'm Chatbot! Ask me about my favorite animal,
color, food, or planet.")

key = input("What is Chatbot's favorite... ")

val = chatbot[key]

print(f"My favorite {key} is {val}!")
```

Make you sure you only ask about categories defined in the dictionary. If you pick something random or there's a typo in your question, Chatbot won't be able to respond. In fact, your program will display an error message.

Enjoy chatting!

YOUR TURN!

Now that you've practiced using dictionaries, see if you can make these changes on your own:

☐ Add a second *input* function after Chatbot's first response. Now, Chatbot can respond a second time! Should you reuse the "key" variable or create a new one?

☐ In between the first and second response, modify some of Chatbot's answers. Now if the user asks about the same category twice, Chatbot will have something different to say!

Pig Latin Translator

LEVEL UP!

Want to learn a "new language" quickly? The rules of Pig Latin are simple. Take the first sound of a word and move it to the back, then add "ay." That first sound is usually one to two letters. For example, the word "fish" becomes:

"ish" + "f" + "ay" = "ishfay"

The word "shark" becomes:

"ark" + "sh" + "ay" = "arkshay"

Using list slicing, we're going to translate English words into Pig Latin! To start, let's create a variable to store our starting English word:

```
eng1 = "frog"
```

Pick any word you like—even the name of a person or place!

In the next line of code, we're going to treat a string like a list of letters. That means the first letter of the string is at index 0. The next is at index 1, etc.

The first sound of the word "frog" is two letters: "f" and "r." These letters are at indices 0 and 1, and we want to send them to the back of the string. So, to start our Pig Latin word, we want all the letters from index 2 and beyond:

```
pig_latin1 = eng1[2:]
```

If the first sound of your word only has one letter–like "fog"–then you'll start from index 1.

Next, we want to add that first sound back to the end of the word. Even though we're treating our string like a list, it's still a string! We can add it to other strings using the + operator:

```
pig_latin1 = eng1[2:] + eng1[:2]
```

Remember that the ending index of a slice isn't included. So "eng1[:2]" will start at the beginning and include every index until 2–which means indices 0 and 1.

Finally, we'll finish our Pig Latin off with the all-important "ay" and print it to the console!

```
pig_latin1 = eng1[2:] + eng1[:2] + "ay"

print(pig_latin1)
```

If you followed the example, you'll see the word "ogfray" in the console!

Let's try with a with a more complicated term that has two words, like "sea turtle!" Both "sea" and "turtle" start with a sound that's only one letter. When we translate that into Pig Latin, it should be "easay urtletay."

Once again, we'll store the English words in a variable:

```
eng2 = "sea turtle"
```

Let's focus on the first word: sea. We want to start with the letters "ea," which are at indices 1 and 2, then add the "s," which is at index 0. Then we'll add an "ay" at the end.

```
pig_latin2 = eng2[1:3] + eng2[0] + "ay"
```

Remember, the last index isn't included in the slice. To include indices 1 and 2, we have to end our slice at index 3.

What about the second word, "turtle"? In our English string, index 3 is a space. Index 4 is a "t," and indices 5 through 9 are "urtle." Let's add these onto our Pig Latin. Don't forget the space in between words!

```
pig_latin2 = eng2[1:3] + eng2[0] + "ay" + " " + eng2[5:10] +
eng2[4] + "ay"
```

Let's go through each slice one at a time: "ea" + "s" + "ay" + " " + "urtle" + "t" + "ay." Try printing it out!

```
print(pig_latin2)
```

You should now see "easay urtletay" in your console!

CODE COMPLETE!

```
eng1 = "frog"

pig_latin1 = eng1[2:] + eng1[:2] + "ay"

print(pig_latin1)

eng2 = "sea turtle"

pig_latin2 = eng2[1:3] + eng2[0] + "ay" + " " + eng2[5:10] +
eng2[4] + "ay"

print(pig_latin2)
```

You now have your own Pig Latin translator. Try it out with your own word suggestions and watch it go!

Now that you've completed this activity, are you ready to play around with more list slicing? Here are some ideas to get you started:

☐ Try writing code for more terms with two words, like "tuna fish" or "blueberry pie," or even your own name!

☐ Use the *input* function and ask your user to choose a word, then use a second *input* function to ask them if the first sound is one or two letters.

☐ Can you write a program that translates Pig Latin back into English?

- -

Data Structures Off-Screen

5

We humans use lots of structures to keep ourselves organized. Think about how you store your clothes. Maybe you have a dresser, or drawers under your bed, or shelves in the closet. Maybe you separate your clothes by type: shirts here, socks there, pants over here. Some people take this a step further and organize their clothes by length or color!

HACKER HINTS:
NAMING YOUR DATA STRUCTURES

Descriptive variable names like "list_of_planets" or "dict_of_telephone_numbers" can be useful, but they're also long and annoying. Often, programmers just use simple plural nouns when naming data structures. Calling a list "planets" hints that it has more than one item. The only downside is that this won't tell you what kind of data structure is being used, such as list or dictionary.

No matter what system you use, the goal is to make things easier to find. Some structures might be more effective than others, but each one has pros and cons, depending on the situation. After all, living out of a suitcase might not be helpful in everyday life, but it's great on vacation!

Coder's Checklist

In this chapter, you learned:

☐ How to create lists and access or change items inside them

☐ That in programming, list indices always start at 0

☐ How to add to and remove from lists

☐ How to slice lists

☐ How to create tuples, and how they're different from lists

☐ How to create dictionaries

That's a lot of new stuff! If you've come this far, you're getting a good handle on the basics of programming. Flip through this chapter anytime you want to review a data structure or two.

6

Conditionals

Conditionals are coding structures that decide which lines of code should be run and which lines should be ignored. Conditionals are also called "branching structures," because they let the program pick one of several options. Picture arriving at an intersection on a street: You can turn right, go straight, or turn left, but you can only pick one direction!

Each "direction" leads the program to a different block of code. Choosing to go right instead of left means the program will behave differently!

Imagine that you're making some dessert. If you make a bowl of ice cream, you'll eat it with a spoon. If you make a milkshake, you'll slurp it up with a straw. And if you want pie, you'll gobble it down with a fork! Your choice—spoon, straw, or fork—depends on the type of dessert you choose. In coding, conditionals allow you to pick the right option. That way, you're not stuck with three utensils or trying to eat ice cream through a straw!

Types of Conditionals

There are several different types of conditionals, depending on how many branches you want in your code.

The **if statement** is a single branch. Picture it as an interesting side street. You can choose to explore it (or not) before coming back to the main code.

The **if-else statement** has two branches, just like a fork in the road! You can either go right or left, but you have to pick one of the two options: if, or else.

The **if-elif-else statement** has as many branches as you want: two, three, ten, or a hundred! This is a useful coding structure when your program needs lots of different options.

How does a conditional choose which branch to explore? It all depends on the **conditions** given to each branch. Let's explore!

(Since the examples in this chapter are a little longer than the ones we've seen before, it's easiest to open a new editor for each section instead of coding in the shell.)

6 Conditions

A **condition** is a Boolean expression used inside a coding structure. In other words, it's a question where the computer can answer "True" or "False." If you want a quick review of Boolean data types, flip back to chapter 4 (page 39).

Each branch of a conditional has its own condition. When the condition is True, we run the code inside the branch. When it's False, we ignore the branch.

The words "conditional" and "condition" sound similar, but they're *very* different things in coding! A conditional is a type of coding structure. A condition, on the other hand, is the Boolean expression used inside that coding structure.

Boolean Expressions

Boolean expressions can use variables, values, and comparison operators like == (the equals-to operator) and != (the not-equals-to operator). The expression is always either "True" or "False."

For example, "4 == 5" is a Boolean expression. In this case, the expression is False, because 4 doesn't equal 5!

When Boolean expressions use variables, the expression might be either "True" or "False," depending on the values inside those variables. Think about this: Does "num_cupcakes == num_guests?" If both variables store the number "5" then the expression is True. If one is "12" and the other is "5," the expression is False.

Here are a few more comparison operators to add to your toolbox:

- \> greater than

- < less than

- \>= greater than or equal to

- <= less than or equal to

Maybe your character needs 100 *or more* coins to get to the next level. Maybe your sprite dies if they have 0 *or less* hit points. With these new operators, you can create more precise conditions. And that means building cooler games and programs!

If Statements

An **if statement** is a simple conditional with only one branch. You can also picture an if statement as a locked box full of code. To unlock the box, the statement's condition must be True. If the condition is False, then the box stays locked and the code inside is never run.

In Python, an if statement looks like this:

```
if coins >= 100:

    print("You made it to the next level!")
```

In this example, the condition is "coins >= 100." If the "coins" variable stores the number 101, then the condition is True, because 101 is greater than or equal to 100. The program runs the print statement and brings the user to the next level!

If "coins" stores the number 89, the condition is False. The program skips the print statement and goes back to the main code.

To write an if statement in Python:

- Start with the "if" keyword, followed by your condition.

- End the line with a colon (:).

- To put code inside the if statement, start the line with either one tab or four spaces. We call this "indenting."

You can put as many lines as you want inside the if statement. However, the moment the program sees a line with no indent, it assumes you've jumped back to the main code.

6 If-Else Statements

The **if-else statement** is a conditional structure with two branches. The first branch is a regular if statement:

```
if is_beach_day:

    print("Put on your swimsuit!")
```

The variable "is_beach_day" stores a Boolean value. It can be either True or False. If it's True, then we unlock the code inside the if statement. If the condition is False, we skip over the print statement and nothing happens.

What if we want something to happen when the condition is False? After all, even if we're not putting on a swimsuit, we need to wear *something*!

To fix this, we can use an else statement:

```
else:

    print("Wear shorts and a t-shirt.")
```

An else statement can only be written directly after an if statement. Together, they create a single conditional.

If the variable "is_beach_day" is storing the value "True" then we run the code inside the if statement. But if "is_beach_day" is False, we run the code inside the else statement. We can only pick one or the other. After all, when you hit a fork in the road, you can't go both left *and* right—you have to choose one.

To test our if-else statement, let's give "is_beach_day" a test value. Add this line of code at the top of your editor:

```
is_beach_day = True
```

All together, the code for your if-else statement should look like this:

```
is_beach_day = True

if is_beach_day:

    print("Put on your swimsuit!")

else:

    print("Wear shorts and a t-shirt.")
```

If you run your code, you'll see "Put on your swimsuit!" in the console. Try changing the value of "is_beach_day" to False and run your code again. Now, you'll see "Wear shorts and a t-shirt."

When we write a conditional, we don't know if its condition will be True or False. The value might depend on a user's choices or on random chance.

Using an if-else statement allows us to plan for different options. If it's sunny? Then you go to the beach. If it's not sunny? Then you stay home and play a board game. Either way, you have a plan!

If–Elif–Else Statements

The **if-elif-else statement** has as many branches as you want. Sometimes, two options aren't enough. Sometimes, you need three, or four, or twenty!

6

To write an if-elif-else statement:

- Start with an if statement. Everything inside the if statement must be indented.

- Directly after the if statement, you can write one or more elif statements. "Elif" is a shortened term for "else if."

- Each elif statement starts with the "elif" keyword, followed by its own condition, then a colon.

- All the code inside an elif statement must be indented.

- You can end your conditional with an else statement, but that's optional. However, you can't put an elif after the else.

Let's try it out! To start, we need an if statement. You can't write an elif without an if! Open up a new editor so your code can start fresh, then write:

```
if is_winter:

    print("Let's build a snowman!")
```

If "is_winter" is True, then we run the code inside the branch and skip the rest of the conditional. If not, we look for other branches and test their conditions.

Now, let's add another branch. Since we've already written an if statement, our next branch must be an elif:

```
elif is_fall:

    print("Let's jump in a pile a leaves!")
```

The elif statement is very similar to the if statement, except that we're using the "elif" keyword instead of "if."

Let's add a third branch:

```
elif is_summer:

    print("Time to throw around a Frisbee!")
```

HACKER HINTS:
TABS VS SPACES

To put a line of code inside an if-elif-else statement, we start that line with an indent. In Python, you can use either one tab or four spaces. But you can't mix and match! If some of your code is indented with spaces, and other parts are indented with tabs, you'll get an error message when you try to run your program.

If we wanted, we could keep adding elifs. A conditional can have as many branches as you want! However, since we're using seasons in our conditions, it makes sense to have four branches—winter, fall, summer, and spring.

Let's end the conditional with an else statement. Coding-wise, this is optional. It's possible to write an if-elif-else statement with no "else."

However, using an else statement makes sense in this case. If it's not winter, fall, or summer, then it definitely has to be spring! There's no day of the year that doesn't have a season. And if we *don't* use an else statement, it's possible that every branch of the conditional could be ignored.

```
else:

    print("Go for a walk, but bring your umbrella!")
```

Let's test our if-elif-else statement. There are three different variables used in the conditions of our branches: "is_winter," "is_fall," and "is_summer." In order to run the code, we need to put test values into these variables. Make sure you define your values before the conditional, not after—otherwise, you'll get an error!

```
is_winter = False

is_fall = True

is_summer = False
```

Your code should look like this:

```python
is_winter = False

is_fall = True

is_summer = False


if is_winter:

    print("Let's build a snowman!")

elif is_fall:

    print("Let's jump in a pile a leaves!")

else:

    print("Go for a walk, but bring your umbrella!")
```

Try running your code. The program starts by checking the condition of the if statement. Since "is_winter" is False, the program moves on to the second branch, "is_fall." Now we have a condition that's True! You should see "Let's jump in a pile of leaves!" printed in your console.

The program won't even bother checking the condition of the third branch, "is_summer." As soon as one condition is True, the rest of the conditional is ignored.

Try changing the values in your variables! What happens when all three of them are False? Play around and see if you can get all four messages printed in your console, one at a time.

What happens if more than one condition is True? Let's try it out:

```python
is_winter = False

is_fall = True

is_summer = True
```

If you run this code, the program will print "Let's jump in a pile of leaves!" Even though the condition "is_summer" is True, that branch comes after "is_fall." When writing your conditional, order matters. No matter how many branches you have, only one of them will be picked. After all, you can't explore two paths at the same time—you'd have to split yourself in half!

Logic Operators

There are three symbols we can use to make more complicated Boolean expressions: *and, or*, and *not*. We call these "logic operators" or "logic symbols."

The **and operator** connects two Boolean expressions into one big mega-expression. For example, if the sky is blue *and* the weather is warm, you'll go outside in a T-shirt. But if the sky is gray or if it's cold, you'll want a jacket.

When using the and operator, *both* mini-expressions must be True in order for the mega-expression to be True. It's all or nothing!

```
if is_sunny and is_warm:

    print("It's t-shirt weather!")
```

To test out this piece of code, let's give "is_sunny" and "is_warm" values. Remember, these must be declared before the conditional:

```
is_sunny = True

is_warm = True
```

If you run your code, you'll see "It's t-shirt weather!" printed in your console. Now, change either "is_sunny" or "is_warm" to False and try again. Nothing appears! Because we used the "and operator," both Boolean expressions must be True.

The **or operator** is the opposite. If *either* mini-expression is True, then the mega-expression is automatically True as well.

```
if is_sunny or is_warm:

    print("Hmmm, still good enough for a t-shirt!")
```

Let's try that out with the following values:

```
is_sunny = True

is_warm = False
```

One of the conditions was True, so text was printed in the console!

Because we used an or operator, only one *or* the other Boolean needed to be True for the whole mega-expression to be True. Even though the weather wasn't warm, it was still sunny.

The only time your condition will be False is when both "is_sunny" and "is_warm" are False. Give the variables new values and see for yourself!

Finally, we have the **not operator**. This operator flips the value of a Boolean expression so that True becomes False and False becomes True.

```
if not is_sunny:

    print("Bring a jacket!")
```

When "is_sunny" is True, "not is_sunny" is False. So when "is_sunny" is False, the condition "not is_sunny" is True. They're always opposites!

To run the code in our if statement, we need "is_sunny" to be False. Give the variable a test value and try it out:

```
is_sunny = False
```

You'll see "Bring a jacket!" printed in the console.

Conditionals in Action

Now that you've learned all about conditionals, let's use them to build fun, interactive programs. With this new tool, your code is no longer one-size-fits-all—it offers choices and different outcomes!

All-or-Nothing Gummy Worms

LEVEL UP!

At a school fair, you and your friend Cory both win packets of delicious gummy worms. To make things interesting, Cory proposes a game of "double or nothing." You'll flip a coin: If it's heads, Cory gives you his gummy worms, but if it's tails, he gets yours!

Let's turn this game into a program using a simple if-else statement.

To start the code, let's ask the user to flip a coin. Then, they can type in the result of the coin toss using the *input* function:

```
coin = input("Flip a coin. Enter 'H' for heads and 'T' for
tails.")
```

There are only two possible values for "coin"—"H" or "T." Let's start by checking if the coin was "heads":

```
if coin == "H":

    print("You win! Enjoy your tasty gummies!")
```

If the coin isn't "heads," then it has to be "tails." In that case, the program skips over the code inside the if statement and goes straight to the else statement:

```
else:

    print("You lose everything!")
```

Flip your coin a few times. Feeling lucky?

CODE COMPLETE!

```python
coin = input("Flip a coin. Enter 'H' for heads and 'T' for
tails.")

if coin == "H":

    print("You win! Enjoy your tasty gummies!")

else:

    print("You lose everything!")
```

Nice job!

But what happens if the user writes something unexpected?

Any input that isn't "H"—whether it's "T," or "24," or even "toaster"—will lead the code into the else statement. Sometimes, this is fine. The program we just wrote will still work and won't crash. However, the outcome of "tails" might seem weird to your user if they typed in "armadillo!"

YOUR TURN!

Now that you've coded this activity, see if you can challenge yourself to make the following changes:

☐ Change your else statement to an elif and use it to check if the coin is "T."
Then, you can use your else statement to catch incorrect input. So if the user types something silly, like "platypus," you can print a funny error message!

☐ Instead of a coin, find a six-sided die. On a 1, 2, or 3, Cory wins, but if the result is greater than 3, then the gummy worms are yours.

☐ Maybe more friends want to join your game! With a six-sided die, you can have up to six winners, which means six branches in your if-elif-else statement. Can you do it?

Roller Coaster Challenge

A group of friends are headed to a theme park. However, some rides (like the Spinning Typhoon and the Rocket Blaster 5000) have a minimum height. Using an if-elif-else statement, let's find the scariest roller coaster that the whole group can ride together.

To start our code, let's put everyone's height (in inches) in a list. The order is completely random:

```
heights = [52, 54, 41, 62, 55, 49, 65]
```

If the shortest person in the group can ride a rollercoaster, then so can everyone else. Since we've stored the heights in a list, we can use the *min* function to find the shortest height:

```
min_height = min(heights)
```

The *min* function returns the smallest number in the list. Then, we store the result in the "min_height" variable.

Time to pick a roller coaster! The three options are:

1. Rumbling Log Ride: no height restrictions

2. Rocket Blaster 5000: 60" and over

3. Spinning Typhoon: 40" and over

When creating our conditional, order matters! Since the friends want to ride the scariest roller coaster possible, we want to start with the ride that has the tallest height requirement: the Rocket Blaster 5000.

```
if min_height >= 60:

    print("You can ride the Rocket Blaster 5000!")
```

If the smallest friend is under 60", the group will have to look for other options. The next scariest roller coaster is the Spinning Typhoon:

```python
elif min_height >= 40:

    print("You can ride the Spinning Typhoon!")
```

If neither of those conditions are True, there's always the roller coaster with no height restriction: the Rumbling Log Ride. Since we're not checking a condition, we can use an else instead of an elif:

```python
else:

    print("You can ride the Rumbling Log Ride!")
```

Our program is done! Make sure that all the lines of code inside your conditionals are indented, and then run your program.

CODE COMPLETE!

```python
heights = [52, 54, 41, 62, 55, 49, 65]

min_height = min(heights)


if min_height >= 60:

    print("You can ride the Rocket Blaster 5000!")

elif min_height >= 40:

    print("You can ride the Spinning Typhoon!")

else:

    print("You can ride the Rumbling Log Ride!")
```

Now, imagine other friends have joined the group, and add and remove other heights to the list to see how it affects your results. Let's see what fun roller coasters the friends can ride together!

Now that you've practiced using if-elif-else statements, see if you can add some new features to the code:

☐ Add one or two new roller coasters to the theme park. Where should you put these new elif statements?

☐ You just discovered a new theme park rule: If you're under 40", you can still ride the Spinning Typhoon if you're accompanied by someone over 66"! Try using logic operators to update your condition!

My New Magical Pet

LEVEL UP!

The owner of a magical pet store wants to help customers choose the perfect pet! To do this, they've created three "yes or no" questions that will help people pick out their very own dragon, phoenix, basilisk, or unicorn.

Using an if-elif-else statement, we'll use the customer's answers to guide them. This is also a great time to use some logic operators!

Let's start our code with three questions printed to the console:

```
print("Are you scared of fire?")

print("Do you like reptiles?")

print("Do you enjoy flying?")
```

Next, let's create variables to store these answers. Because each answer is "yes or no," we'll use Boolean data types.

You can answer these questions yourself *or* use random "placeholders" like the values below. In real life, the values would be different for each customer and we wouldn't know what they are in advance! Plus, we'd use the *input* function to ask our users! For now, though, let's "hard code" some answers and write them directly into the code, like so:

```
scared_of_fire = True

likes_reptiles = True

likes_flying = False
```

When creating our guide, it's best to start with the trickier pets! A good future dragon owner would answer "False" to "scared_of_fire," "True" to "likes_reptiles," and "True" to "likes_flying." It won't work with any other combination! For a unicorn, on the other hand, none of those answers really matter.

So let's start with the dragon:

```
if not scared_of_fire and likes_reptiles and likes_flying:

    print("You should get a dragon!")
```

We connect our Booleans with and operators because all three of these need to be True. If even one is False—if an owner is scared of fire or doesn't like reptiles—then adopting a dragon is a bad idea, right?

Notice how the not operator is in front of "scared_of_fire." That's because we want "scared_of_fire" to be False, but the condition as a whole to be True!

Next, let's add a phoenix to our guide. Since phoenixes are birds made out of fire, a future phoenix owner should answer "False" to "scared_of_fire" and "True" to "likes_flying."

Remember, another person's answers might be different than your own! Right now our variables have "dummy" (random) values, but those values could be changed at any time.

```
elif not scared_of_fire and likes_flying:

    print("You should get a phoenix!")
```

Since a phoenix isn't a reptile, it doesn't matter if a user "likes_reptiles." But what about basilisks? Now, "like_reptiles" is very important. Flying and fire, not so much.

```
elif likes_reptiles:

    print("You should get a basilisk!")
```

Finally, all that's left is the unicorn. Should we use an else statement or an elif?

```
else:
    print("You should get a unicorn!")
```

All done! With this handy guide, everyone can find their perfect magical pet. Try rearranging your code to make it a little easier to read.

CODE COMPLETE!

```
print("Are you scared of fire?")
scared_of_fire = True


print("Do you like reptiles?")
likes_reptiles = True


print("Do you enjoy flying?")
likes_flying = False


if not scared_of_fire and likes_reptiles and likes_flying:
    print("You should get a dragon!")
elif not scared_of_fire and likes_flying:
    print("You should get a phoenix!")
elif likes_reptiles:
    print("You should get a basilisk!")
else:
    print("You should get a unicorn!")
```

Should *you* adopt the dragon, phoenix, basilisk, or unicorn? Try it and see, then have fun with your new magical pet!

YOUR TURN!

Are you ready for a challenge? Using your new skills with logic operators and conditionals, see if you can make some changes to your code:

☐ With three different answers, each True or False, there are eight possible combinations. Try adding a few of your own magical pets to the guide!

☐ Instead of assigning "True" or "False" values to your variables, use the *input* function to ask the user. This will make the guide interactive! Remember, the *input* function only returns strings, so you'll have to update your conditions to test if the strings are "yes" or "no." For example, "if is_scared_of_fire" would become "if is_scared_of_fire == "yes"."

Conditionals Off-Screen

Have you ever made a plan and then had it go wrong? Maybe you tried to bake cookies, then realized you didn't have any eggs. Or maybe you headed to the beach and got stuck in a rainstorm.

When things like this happen, you start making backup plans. You've identified the important variables—eggs, sunny weather, etc. These are the things that decide if Plan A will happen. And in a worst-case scenario, you can always make a Plan B!

Conditionals are a way of structuring choices. They're not the choices themselves, but the ability to choose between different options, based on unpredictable variables. If you have eggs, then you make cookies. If you don't have eggs, then you make pudding. The condition is whether or not you have eggs. The conditional is the question—should I do this or that, and why?

See if you can notice some conditionals in your own daily life!

HACKER HINTS:
VALIDATING USER INPUT

"Validating" input means checking that your user didn't type something silly into the *input* function. Often, we use if-else statements to see if the user's answer matched our question. If you ask for a phone number and the user types "orangutan," it could lead to problems in your code!

Coder's Checklist

In this chapter, you learned:

☐ How to write if statements

☐ What Boolean expressions are

☐ How to use comparison operators like >=, >, <=, and < in Boolean expressions, as well as != and ==

☐ What logical operators are (and, or, not)

☐ How to use elif and else statements

☐ How to choose the order of your conditions in an if-elif-else statement

These chapters aren't going anywhere—they're here for you! If you ever want to review these concepts, flip back to the start of the chapter.

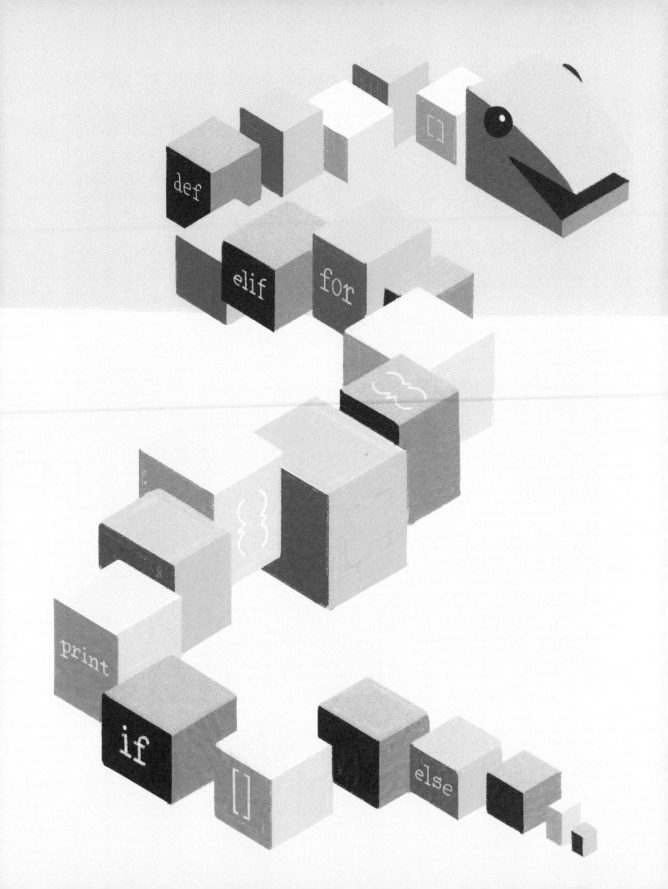

7

Loops

A **loop** is a coding structure that's used to repeat specific lines of code. It's basically a shortcut. Picture a boring task, like scanning 100 pieces of paper. Wouldn't it be cool if you could just scan one piece of paper and the rest scanned themselves automatically? Using a loop, you can!

Loops save coders a lot of time. They also keep your code consistent. If you're doing a boring task over and over, you're more likely to make mistakes. When you use a loop, the task can be performed exactly the same way each time. All 100 pieces of paper are guaranteed to be scanned perfectly!

There are two main types of loops: **while loops**, which have a variable (changing) number of rounds, and **for loops**, which have a fixed (unchanging) number of rounds.

While Loops

A **while loop** is a loop that uses a condition. As long as the condition is True, the while loop keeps going. When the condition becomes False, the loop ends. Think of them like this: *while* the condition is true, the loop keeps right on going. There! Much easier to remember, right?

To write a while loop:

- Start with the "while" keyword.

- Next, write your condition. Just like an if statement, the condition is a Boolean expression.

- Finish the line off with a colon (:).

- To put a line of code inside the while loop, start it with an indent.

Here's a simple example. Try this code out in a new editor:

```python
while is_hungry:

    print("Have a snack!")
```

Our condition is "is_hungry." This is a Boolean variable. As long it stores the value "True," the loop will keep going and we'll keep printing "Have a snack!" over and over.

To run this code, let's give "is_hungry" a test value. Don't forget to define this variable before the loop! And don't run your code just yet . . .

```python
is_hungry = True
```

We have a small problem. The value of "is_hungry" never gets changed, so the while loop's condition is always True. The loop never stops and we'll be stuck eating snacks forever!

To fix this, we need a way to change the value of "is_hungry" inside our while loop. One option is to ask the user using the *input* function:

```python
q = input("Are you still hungry? Enter Y or N: ")
```

Then, using an if statement, we can update "is_hungry":

```python
if q == "N":

    is_hungry = False
```

We have to be careful about our indentation here. Since the if statement is inside the while loop, we should start the if statement with an indent.

The line "is_hungry = False" is inside the if statement and also inside the while loop. So that line should start with two indents!

Everything should line up in your editor just like this:

```python
is_hungry = True

while is_hungry:

    print("Have a snack!")

    q = input("Are you still hungry? Enter Y or N: ")

    if q == "N":

        is_hungry = False
```

Try running the code now. See how the same lines are repeated over and over in your console, right up until you type "N?"

You can put conditionals inside loops, loops inside conditionals, and loops inside other loops. Sometimes, you'll even have lines of code with three or four indents! Before running your code, first double-check that everything lines up in your editor. A line of code should always be one indent farther than the "for," "while," or "if" keyword of the structure it's inside.

Counting Laps

Another way to avoid infinite while loops is to use a "counter variable." Starting at 1, this variable counts the number of "laps" you've run around your loop. Then, in your condition, you can set the limit.

Picture riding your favorite roller coaster. Let's start our counter variable at lap number one:

```python
num_laps = 1
```

Maybe the roller coaster goes around the track five times before stopping. In that case, we'd write our while loop like this:

```python
while num_laps <= 5:
```

As long as we haven't done more than five laps, the condition is True and the code inside the while loop repeats. To avoid an infinite loop, we need to update the value of "num_laps" inside the body of the loop. Let's use the plus-equal operator (+=) to increase the value of "num_laps" by one with each lap:

```python
print(f"Here goes lap #{num_laps}!")
num_laps += 1
```

Try running this in your console! See how the value of "num_laps" starts at 1, then increases to 2, then 3, all the way to 5?

While loops are used when you don't know how many rounds you need. Depending on the user's choices, the while loop can run once, twice, or a thousand times! Most computer games, for example, are built using while loops. The game runs until the user wins, loses, or gets bored and stops the game.

7

HACKER HINTS:
INFINITE WHILE LOOPS

If you find yourself stuck in a while loop, don't worry! It's a common bug for all programmers. There are several ways to stop a runaway program. Many IDEs have a "Stop" button next to the "Run" button. If not, you can type CTRL+C to interrupt the program. In IDLE, you can also click "Shell" and then "Restart Shell."

While loops with counters are useful if you're changing the value of the counter inside the loop. Maybe the counter resets to "0" if the user finds a magic item inside a game. But if you simply need a fixed number of rounds, you're better off using a for loop. Read on to learn how!

For Loops

For loops are another type of loop. You can think of them as while loops with built-in counters! For loops are only meant to last *for* a set amount of time–get it? Instead of repeating code until a condition becomes False, for loops are programmed to repeat exactly 5, or 10, or 100 times. Just like setting a timer!

To code a for loop in Python, we need to use the *range* function:

```
range(10)
```

Like other functions such as *print*, *input*, and *min*, *range* uses round brackets. In this example, the function creates a sequence of 10 numbers. Like lists, this sequence starts at 0, which means the last number of the range is 9. The number you put inside the round brackets is never included in the range.

So, to create a sequence of numbers from 0 to 4, we'd write:

```
range(5)
```

Picture the *range* function as your timer, counting the laps one by one. To write a for loop:

- Start with the "for" keyword.

- Next, put the name of your "counter" variable. This is a new variable created just for the loop.

- Add the "in" keyword.

- Finish with the *range* function and end the line with a colon.

Let's create a for loop to count while you run 10 laps around a track:

```
for x in range(10):
```

In this example, our counter variable is called "x." We can picture "range(10)" as a timer set to 10 laps. The counter "x" is the clock hand counting the laps one by one.

On the first lap, the value of "x" is 0. On the second lap, it's 1. At every lap, the value increases by 1, until we reach the end of the timer at 9.

If this seems a bit confusing, go back and review the example with the while loop and the counter, on page 97. The two loops work the same way, with one key difference. In the while loop, we increased "counter" by hand, while "x" increases automatically in the for loop.

```
for x in range(10):

    print(f"Running lap #{x}")
```

You can't change the value of "x" inside a for loop, but you can still access it. For example, you could use it in an if statement:

```
for x in range(10):

    if x == 9:

        print("Almost there! Last lap...")

    print(f"Running lap #{x}")
```

In this example, we check if the counter variable "x" currently stores the value 9. Since the value of "x" changes every round, this condition will only be True once—on the final lap!

For loops are useful when you know ahead of time how many rounds you need. Maybe you're going through a list with 10 items. Or maybe you're playing a game with exactly three rounds.

Because the counter variable is updated automatically, you can't update it yourself. If you set the timer for 10 rounds, you're getting exactly 10 rounds—no more and no less!

For Each Loops

With for loops, we set the number of rounds in advance. This makes them the perfect tool for working with lists.

There's even a special type of for loop called the **for each loop**. You can use it to access each item in a list, one at a time.

As an example, let's start with a list of pet names, stored as strings:

```
pet_names = ["Mr. Whiskers", "Snickerdoodle", "Mittens",
"Lucky", "Sergeant Wiggles", "Mustard"]
```

The for each loop would like this:

```
for pet in pet_names:
```

You're still using the "for" and "in" keywords, as well as a colon. But instead of the *range* function, just put the name of a list!

Normally, counter variables like "x" store numbers. However, the variable "pet" is going to store pet names. On the first round of the loop, "pet" will store the value "Mr. Whiskers." On the second round, it will store "Snickerdoodle." One pet at a time, we'll go through the entire list until we reach "Mustard."

7

```
for pet in pet_names:

    print(f"{pet} is a good pet!")
```

It doesn't matter if you make the list longer or shorter. For each loops always go through a list's items one at a time, front to back, until they've seen every item.

Loops in Action

Mastering loops opens up a whole world of cool new programs! Let's see what we can build with our newest tool.

My Python Snake

LEVEL UP!

Some snakes are short, while other snakes are very, very long. Using a for loop, let's print one in the console!

To start, pick a length for your slithery friend. Make sure it's an integer!

```
length = 10
```

Your snake will be built out of letters, numbers, and symbols. You can create the head, body, and tail like this:

```
head = ">-( 0)"

body = "     |"

tail = "     __/"
```

See how the ">-" creates a forked tongue, the "0" makes the eye, and the round brackets make up the snake's head?

The body is a little bit tricky. To make things line up, you'll need to add five spaces in front of the "|" symbol. Same with the tail: first five spaces, then two underscores (_), and finally one backslash (/).

Now, let's print the head to the console:

```
print(head)
```

To print the body, let's use a for loop:

```
for x in range(length):
    print(body)
```

Remember how the *range* function is like a timer? We've set it to the value stored in "length." In the example, that's 10. Since ranges start at 0, "range(10)" will create a sequence of numbers from 0 to 9. At each round, the loop prints a new segment of the snake's body.

Exit the loop and finish by printing the tail in the console. Make sure you *don't* indent this line of code. Otherwise, it'll repeat at every round of the loop.

```
    print(tail)
```

Run your program and you'll see a slithering snake in your console—your very own "Python" friend!

CODE COMPLETE!

```
length = 10

head = ">-( 0)"

body = "     |"

tail = "     __/"


print(head)

for x in range(length):
    print(body)
print(tail)
```

Play around with different lengths. What does a snake look like with no body? Can you make a snake so long that it crashes your program? Try it out—it's all part of experimenting!

YOUR TURN!

Now that you've completed this activity, challenge yourself to make the following changes to your code. Feel free to flip back through the chapter if you want to review a concept:

☐ Instead of printing the snake's body, print the counter variable "x." You'll get a snake made out of numbers!

☐ Using the *input* function, ask the user for the length of the snake. Don't forget to convert this into an int.

☐ Try creating the same program using a while loop instead of a for loop. The for loop is the better tool for this situation, but it's still good to practice both!

Who's Getting Splashed?

LEVEL UP!

It's a hot summer day, but you know just how to cool off—with a fun game of water balloon toss! Your friends and family stand in a circle. Each person throws the balloon to the person next to them. It could pop at any moment! Using a for loop, let's find out who gets soaked.

To start, create a list of friends and/or family:

```
friends = ["Laura", "Chloe", "Eric", "Gabriel", "Betty",
"Elise", "Brendan", "Jon", "Amanda", "Grant"]
```

Next, we'll declare a variable to choose who pops the balloon. Pick any random integer that's shorter than the length of your list. So if your list has 10 people, you can't pick a number higher than 9, but it's okay to pick 0. No peeking!

```
pop_num = 6
```

The person at position 6 is going to get soaked. Let's find out who it is!

Because our program uses a list, it seems like a good time to use a for each loop. However, we need a counter variable to help us find the person at position 6. So let's use a regular for loop instead:

```
for i in range(10):
```

The counter variable is called "i" because we're using it to check indices in a list.

Next, we use "range(10)" because the example list has 10 people. Your list might be shorter or longer.

Inside the for loop, use an if statement to check if we've reached the position where the water balloon pops:

```
if i == pop_num:
```

If so, print the name of the person who got soaked! Do you remember how to access an item from a list? (Hint: We need square brackets and the item's position.)

```
soaked = friends[i]
```

```
print(f"The water balloon was popped by {soaked}!")
```

Run your program to see who's the unlucky friend!

CODE COMPLETE!

```
friends = ["Laura", "Chloe", "Eric", "Gabriel", "Betty",
"Elise", "Brendan", "Jon", "Amanda", "Grant"]

pop_num = 6


for i in range(10):

    if i == pop_num:

        soaked = friends[i]

print(f"The water balloon was popped by {soaked}!")
```

Now that you've popped one water balloon, try playing around with different integers. This is great practice for both loops and lists.

YOUR TURN!

Now that you've coded this activity, see if you can challenge yourself to make the following changes:

☐ Add an else statement that contains another print message. Print the names of everyone who caught the water balloon successfully.

☐ When someone gets soaked, remove them from the list. This is a little bit tricky, because you remove a friend using their name, not their position! (Hint: Store the friend's name in a new variable.)

☐ With one friend eliminated, add another round to the game of water balloon toss. You won't need a new list, but you'll need a new random number and a new for loop. What should be different about this new for loop?

- -

Find the Buried Treasure

LEVEL UP! ▪▪▪

A crew of pirates are searching for buried treasure along the shore! To make sure they don't accidentally miss any treasure, they've separated the beach into 100 sections and given each one a number from 1 to 100. After searching a section, they'll know if that section's number was "too high" or "too low," an important clue that will help them find the real location of the treasure! Then, they'll try again at a new section of the beach.

Using a while loop and some if statements, let's turn this treasure hunt into an interactive game!

To start, let's pick a position for the treasure. This can be any number between 0 and 100:

```
treasure_pos = 86
```

Next, let's give the user some instructions, then ask them to guess the position of the treasure. Since the *input* function always returns a string, we need to convert the value into an int:

```
print("Guess the location of the buried treasure!")

guess = input("Enter a number between 0 and 100: ")

guess = int(guess)
```

At the start of the game, we don't know how many guesses the user will need. Maybe they'll guess right away. Maybe they'll need 99 guesses! Because we don't know, it's best to use a while loop.

The game continues as long as "guess" and "treasure_pos" don't match. To check this, we can use the not-equals-to operator (!=). This means our condition is:

```
while guess != treasure_pos:
```

If the user guesses correctly, then "guess" will equal "treasure_pos." The two variables will no longer be different, the condition will become False, and the loop will end. So our loop only runs while the user makes *incorrect* guesses.

There's just one small problem. We want our *input* function to be *inside* the while loop so the user can guess multiple times. Unless the user is very lucky, they'll need more than one guess!

So let's move the guessing lines inside the while loop. Problem solved!

```
while guess != treasure_pos:

    guess = input("Enter a number between 0 and 100: ")

    guess = int(guess)
```

Except there's a new problem. The first time we check the while loop's condition, the "guess" variable doesn't have a value, since no one's guessed anything yet.

We can solve this by giving the "guess" variable a dummy (random) value to get the while loop started. Add this line to the top of your code editor:

```
guess = -1
```

The next step is to tell the user if their guess was "too high" or "too low." We can do this with an if statement:

```python
if guess > treasure_pos:

    print("Too high!")
```

We're putting a conditional inside a while loop, so make sure your if statement has one indent, and your print statement has two.

Next, let's check if the guess was too low:

```python
elif guess < treasure_pos:

    print("Too low!")
```

Now, what happens if the user guesses correctly, and "guess == treasure_pos"? Neither of the conditions are True, so nothing is printed to the console.

However, on the next round of the loop, the program will check the while loop's condition. That condition is "guess != treasure_pos," which is True when the guesses are *different*. If "guess" matches "treasure_pos," the while loop's condition becomes False. The treasure has been discovered and the program automatically leaves the loop.

Once we've exited, finish your program by congratulating the user:

```python
print(f"Congratulations! You found the treasure buried at
position {treasure_pos}!")
```

Run your code and test it out!

CODE COMPLETE!

```python
treasure_pos = 86

guess = -1
```

```
print("Guess the location of the buried treasure!")


while guess != treasure_pos:

    guess = input("Enter a number between 0 and 100: ")

    guess = int(guess)

    if guess > treasure_pos:

        print("Too high!")

    elif guess < treasure_pos:

        print("Too low!")


print(f"Congratulations! You found the treasure buried at
position {treasure_pos}!")
```

You can challenge friends or family to find the buried treasure. How many guesses do you think they'll need?

YOUR TURN!

Now that you've practiced using while loops, see if you can make the following changes on your own:

☐ Using a list, keep track of the user's guesses. Print these to the console so the user can see what numbers they've already tried. (Hint: Start with an empty list, then append guesses to it inside the loop.)

☐ Try giving your user only seven guesses. The easiest way to do this is to create a new variable (maybe "num_guesses_left") and tweak your while loop's condition. (Hint: Check out the section "Logic Operators" on page 83.)

Loops Off-Screen

Loops allow you to write your code once, then repeat it as many times as you like. If you look at the world around you, you'll see lots of machines that do this.

Picture a sewing machine. It does one thing: make a tiny, perfect stitch. Then, it repeats this action over and over. Using a sewing machine is way faster than doing all those stitches by hand and the result has fewer mistakes!

Think about it. What are some other long, boring tasks that humans have made faster and better by using loops?

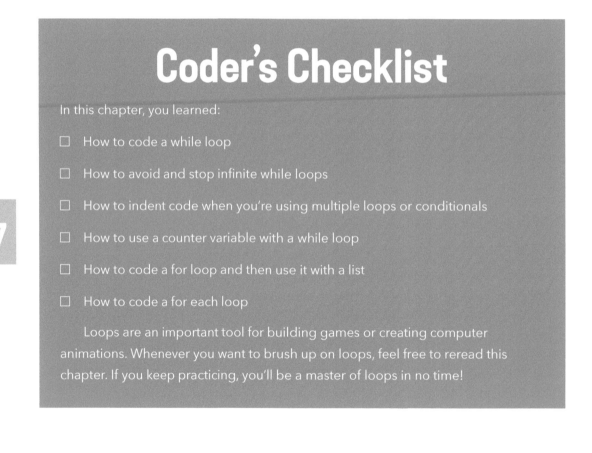

Coder's Checklist

In this chapter, you learned:

- ☐ How to code a while loop

- ☐ How to avoid and stop infinite while loops

- ☐ How to indent code when you're using multiple loops or conditionals

- ☐ How to use a counter variable with a while loop

- ☐ How to code a for loop and then use it with a list

- ☐ How to code a for each loop

Loops are an important tool for building games or creating computer animations. Whenever you want to brush up on loops, feel free to reread this chapter. If you keep practicing, you'll be a master of loops in no time!

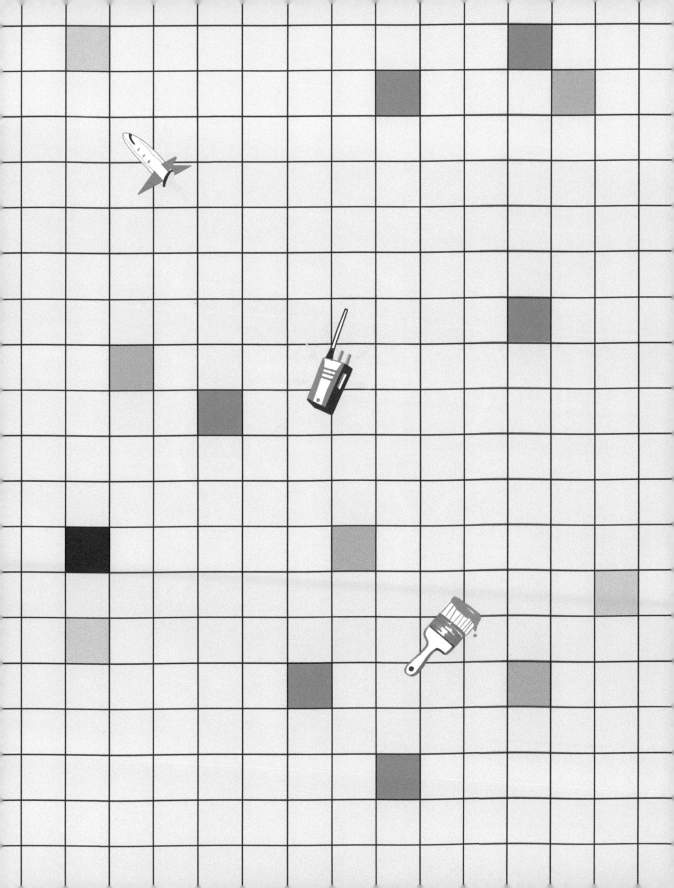

8

Functions

A **function** is a block of code that completes a specific task. We can define them ourselves or use functions created by other programmers.

When you have a big project, it's best to split up the work. If you're throwing a birthday party, maybe one person buys decorations, one person creates party games, and one person bakes a cake. If you're camping, you might split up who starts the fire, who makes dinner, and who sets up the tent.

Similarly, anytime you have a big program, it's best to split it up into functions. Picture each function as a tiny helper robot. The robot is only good at one task. Whenever you need help with that one task, the robot swoops in and takes care of it!

Splitting up your program into functions keeps your code neat and organized. And because you can reuse functions, you don't have to code the same task twice.

Parts of a Function

To create a function, we need to know:

- The name of the function we will create.

- **Input**: What information, or tools, does the function need to complete its task? A robot that cleans your house needs a broom. A robot baking a cake needs eggs, flour, and butter.

- **Output**: What does the finished task look like? Is it a clean house? A delicious cake?

In chapter 1, we talked about the input and output of programs. The difference between functions and programs is really about size. Programs are big, vague projects like "throwing a birthday party." Functions are small, specific tasks like "baking a cake."

Let's start with a small function. When we define our own functions, we use the "def" keyword:

```
def bake_cake():

    print("Time to bake a cake!")
```

In this case, the function's name is "bake_cake." It doesn't have any input or output. It just prints the words "Time to bake a cake!" whenever we ask.

To write a function in Python:

- Start with the "def" keyword.

- Next, write the name of your function.

- Then, put a pair of round brackets: ( ).

- Finish off the line with a colon.

To put code inside a function, start the line with an indent, just like loops and if-elif-else statements!

Next, let's add some input. Functions receive input through **parameters**. A parameter is a special variable that's defined inside a function's round brackets. When it's time to run the function, we put values inside the function's parameters. Then, those values can be accessed inside the function.

Let's say we're creating a "cake baking" function. We want the function to bake all kinds of cakes: red velvet, black forest, vanilla sprinkle. To make this happen, we'll create a "cake_type" parameter.

When it's time to bake a cake, we'll specify which flavor we want. If we want a chocolate cake, we put the value "chocolate" inside "cake_type." If we want a coffee cake, then we put the value "coffee" inside instead.

The result looks like this:

```
def bake_cake(cake_type):

    print(f"Time to bake a {cake_type} cake!")
```

In the first line of this code block, we define our "bake_cake" function with one parameter inside the round brackets: "cake_type." In the second line, we print an f-string that uses the value inside "cake_type." So if "butter pecan" is stored inside "cake_type," the function will print "Time to bake a butter pecan cake!"

A function can have as many parameters as you want: zero, two, ten—whatever. They all go inside the round brackets, separated by commas. For example, if we want to add a "cake_size" parameter, we'd define the function like this:

```
def bake_cake(cake_type, cake_size):

    print(f"Time to bake a {cake_size} {cake_type} cake!")
```

8

Remember, parameters can only be accessed inside the function that defines them. Think of them like variables that only exist inside a function.

If you're writing this code in your editor, you might notice nothing happens when you run the code! Why isn't the print statement showing up in the console?

When you define a function, you're teaching the "helper robot" how to do its task. But until you actually give it a command, it's just going to stand there, waiting. We'll talk more about "calling functions" in one of the next sections, when we'll actually use our functions. This is also the step where we put values inside the parameters.

Return Values

After a function completes its task, it can output its result using the "return" keyword. When you call a function, the program starts running the lines of code inside it. The function ends once it returns:

```python
def bake_cake(cake_type, cake_size):

    print(f"Time to bake a {cake_size} {cake_type} cake!")

    return f"A {cake_size} {cake_type} cake"
```

Notice the new line at the end of the function? In this example, we're returning an f-string. If "cake_type" stores the value "chocolate," and "cake_size" stores the value "large," our return value will be "A large chocolate cake."

You can return any data type: integers, strings, Booleans, floats. Pretty handy! Let's take a look at another function:

```python
def hot_chocolate_calculator(num_people):

    print("How many cups of water do I need for {num_people} people?")

    return num_people * 1.5
```

The "hot_chocolate_calculator" function returns a float. If we're making hot chocolate for four people, we'll place the value "4" inside "num_people." Since we need 1.5 cups for each serving, the return value of the function would be 6. That's how many cups of water we should boil!

Once a function returns a value, the function ends. If there are lines of code after the return statement, they'll be ignored.

Not all functions return values, and functions that print or display information often don't. You only need to return values if you plan to use those values later in your program.

Calling Functions

So far we've built our "helper robots" and given them instructions to complete specific tasks. Now, let's see them in action! To call a function and get it running, write the function's name. Then, put values inside the function's parameters. We call this "passing" values to a function:

```
bake_cake("rainbow", "large")
```

The values "rainbow" and "large" are called **arguments**. An argument is a special term for a value stored inside a parameter.

The number of parameters and their order are found inside a function's definition. Let's take a look at the line where we define "bake_cake":

```
def bake_cake(cake_type, cake_size):
```

You can see that function "bake_cake" has two parameters: "cake_type" and "cake_size." When we called "bake_cake," we put the value "rainbow" into the variable "cake_type" and "large" into the variable "cake_size."

Try running your code! You should now see text appear in your console.

What if we call the function with its arguments in a different order?

```
bake_cake("large", "rainbow")
```

Now the value "large" is inside "cake_type" and "rainbow" is inside "cake_size." That's no good! Our code will still run, because both parameters take string arguments. But in other functions, mixing up the order of parameters will make your code crash. That's why it's important to check a function's definition before calling it. Make sure the parameters are in the right order and that you're not forgetting one.

The cool thing about functions is that we can call them over and over again. Let's call "bake_cake" with different arguments:

```
bake_cake("rainbow", "large")

bake_cake("coffee", "small")

bake_cake("maple walnut", "extra large")
```

8

If you run this code, you'll see three different lines of text in your console. See how passing different arguments to "bake_cake" led to different results?

Let's go over all the code in your editor:

```python
def bake_cake(cake_type, cake_size):

    print(f"Time to bake a {cake_size} {cake_type} cake!")

    return f"A {cake_size} {cake_type} cake"

bake_cake("rainbow", "large")

bake_cake("coffee", "small")

bake_cake("maple walnut", "extra large")
```

The top three lines are the function's definition. This is where you teach your "helper robot" how to bake a cake. The last three lines are function calls. This is where you tell your robot what kind of cake to bake (large rainbow, small coffee, or extra large maple walnut) and the robot goes off, bakes a cake, and returns it to you!

Next, we'll use variables to collect return values:

```python
cake = bake_cake("rainbow", "large")
```

The value returned by the "bake_cake" function will be "A large rainbow cake." This string is now stored in the variable "cake." We can do whatever we want with it–print it, add it to other strings, multiply it with integers.

We can also collect values that aren't strings! Let's call the "hot_chocolate _calculator" function from earlier and store its return value in a new variable:

```python
num_cups = hot_chocolate_calculator(4)

print(f"We need {num_cups} cups of water")
```

The return value of "6" was stored in "num_cups," which we printed to the console using an f-string. If we give "hot_chocolate_calculator" a different input, then we'll get a different output:

```
num_cups = hot_chocolate_calculator(1)

print(f"We need {num_cups} cups of water")
```

Functions allow us to reuse code. And because we can change the values inside a function's parameters, we can get thousands of different results!

Using Python's Built-In Functions

We've compared functions to "helper robots" and learned how to build and use our own. Python also comes with built-in "helper robots!" These are functions that are written by professional programmers and installed in the language.

You've actually used some of these built-in functions before! Remember *print* and *input*? Both of these are built-in functions. You've also used *min*, which takes a list as a parameter and returns the smallest value in the list. Not to mention *range*, *append*, and *remove*. Let's take a look at a few more useful functions!

Len Function

The *len* function is used to calculate the length of a list or a tuple. Does the list have five items? 500? It doesn't matter—*len* saves you the trouble of having to count it yourself!

Input: A list or tuple
Output: The length of that list/tuple
Let's start by defining a list:

```
camping_activities = ["hiking", "biking", "canoeing",
"roasting marshmallows"]
```

Next, we'll use the *len* function to calculate the length of the list and store the result in a variable:

```
length = len(camping_activities)

print(length)
```

8

Try adding and removing items from the list and see how the result of len changes!

Sorted Function

The *sorted* function is used to sort the items inside lists. If you're sorting a list of integers, they'll be sorted from smallest to largest. If you're sorting a list of strings, they'll be sorted alphabetically.

Input: A list
Output: A new, sorted list
Let's make a quick list of integers:

```
x = [0, 7, 3, 10, 1, 4, 2, 8]
```

Now let's sort it and store the result in a new variable:

```
y = sorted(x)

print(y)
```

Let's try sorting a list of strings and print out the result:

```
camping_activities = ["hiking", "biking", "canoeing",
"roasting marshmallows"]

sorted_activities = sorted(camping_activities)

print(sorted_activities)
```

Choice Function

The *choice* function picks a random item from a list or tuple. Picture a blindfolded person choosing a random item from a bag. Who knows which item will be picked? Nobody!

Input: A list or tuple
Output: One random item

Using the *choice* function is a bit different than using *print*, *input*, *sorted*, or *len*. Those functions are built into the core Python language. *Choice*, on the other hand, is stored in a **library**. Libraries are folders full of code that contain lots of useful helper functions. Each library specializes in something different.

To use the *choice* function in our code, we need to import it. This is like heading to the library, borrowing a book, and then bringing it home:

```
from random import choice
```

Write this line at the very top of your code file. "Random" is the name of the library, and "choice" is the name of the function we're borrowing.

Let's try it out! First, we need to create a list:

```
costume_ideas = ["witch", "vampire", "giant pumpkin",
"dinosaur", "ballerina", "pirate", "astronaut"]
```

Now, let's use the *choice* function to select one costume at random:

```
costume = choice(costume_ideas)

print(costume)
```

Try running this bit of code a few times. See how *choice* keeps selecting different costumes?

HACKER HINTS:
CONTROL FLOW

Programs usually read lines of code from top to bottom. When the program sees a function call, however, it jumps to the first line of the function. Then it goes through the function's lines of code one at a time, top to bottom. When the function returns a value, the program goes back to where it left off. Sort of like pausing a movie, going to make popcorn, and then coming back to your movie!

8

Functions in Action

We've learned how to define functions and use them in our code. Let's see how powerful this new tool is by testing it out!

Quest for the Biggest Jellyfish!

LEVEL UP!

A group of explorers are trying to find the biggest jellyfish in the world!

To help them, a team of top scientists have figured out how to guess a jellyfish's size based on how deep the water is. Let's turn this into a simple function called "jellyfish_size_guesser."

Input: How deep is the water, in miles (a float)

Output: How big is the jellyfish, in feet (also a float)

Let's start by defining our function:

```python
def jellyfish_size_guesser(water_depth):
```

Don't forget the colon at the end of the line!

Now, it's time to put the scientists' equation inside our function. The deeper the water, the bigger the jellyfish. The math goes something like this:

```python
jellyfish_size = 28 * water_depth + 0.1
```

Let's finish our function with a return statement:

```python
return jellyfish_size
```

Remember, our function won't do anything unless we call it. What value should we pass to the "water_depth" parameter? Well, a 10-story building is about 100 feet high, or 0.02 miles. Let's start with that:

```python
size = jellyfish_size_guesser(0.02)

print(size)
```

Did you get 0.66? That's just over 7 inches. So if you swam 100 feet deep, you might find a jellyfish the size of your hand.

CODE COMPLETE!

```
def jellyfish_size_guesser(water_depth):

    jellyfish_size = 28 * water_depth + 0.1

    return jellyfish_size

size = jellyfish_size_guesser(0.02)

print(size)
```

Play around with different values to see what you get. The Marianas Trench, which is the deepest part of the ocean, is almost 7 miles deep! What size jellyfish could you find there? Do you think that's where the largest jellyfish can be found?

YOUR TURN!

Now that you've written a function, challenge yourself to make some changes to it:

☐ The explorers want the height of the jellyfish in inches, not feet. How can you change your return value to make this possible? (Hint: There are 12 inches in a foot.)

☐ Use the *input* function to make your program interactive: Ask the user for the depth of the water! And don't forget to convert their answer into an int.

☐ What if the user types something that doesn't make sense, like "-10 miles"? That value is impossible! Add an if statement inside your function that checks if the value inside "water_depth" is greater than 0. What should happen if it isn't? Should you print an error message?

Anagram Checker

Pick a word, any word! If you can rearrange its letters into a new word, then you've found an anagram. "RATS," for example, is an anagram of "STAR." So is "ARTS."

To check if two words are anagrams, let's define a simple "is_anagram" function. We'll practice defining functions, use Python's built-in *sorted* method, and review conditionals.

First, let's figure out our input and output:

Input: Two words that could be anagrams (each is a string).

Output: A Boolean value that's True if the words are anagrams, and False if they're not.

Since our function has two parameters, let's separate them with a comma. We're defining a function, so we put variable names, not values:

```
def is_anagram(word1, word2):
```

How can we tell if two words are anagrams? Let's look at an example: "STAR" and "RATS." If we sort the letters of each word alphabetically, "STAR" becomes "ARST." "RATS" also becomes "ARST." The two results match!

Since anagrams are different words that use the same letters, if you sort the letters of any two anagrams, the results will always be the same. So, we can use the *sorted* function inside our "is_anagram" function to check if the values of "word1" and "word2" are anagrams. We'll sort the letters in each word, and if they match, then we've found a pair of anagrams.

Remember how strings can be treated like lists of letters? Let's see what happens if we pass a string to the *sorted* function. You can try this code out in your IDLE shell:

```
sorted("STAR")
```

The letters have been sorted into "ARST!" However, the result is a list of letters, not a string.

Back inside our "is_anagram" function, let's use an if statement to compare our two lists of sorted letters:

```
if sorted(word1) == sorted(word2):

    return True
```

If "word1" is "STAR," then "sorted(word1)" is "ARST." If "word2" is "RATS," then "sorted(word2)" is also "ARST." Using the equals-to operator (==), we compare the letters in these two sorted words.

Does "ARST" == "ARST?" It does! The sorted letters match, meaning "STAR" and "RATS" are anagrams.

When we define a function, we don't know what values will be given to "word1" and "word2." Maybe they're anagrams, maybe not. That's why we sort the letters and use an if statement to check! If the letters match, we return "True." If they don't, we return "False."

Let's add an else statement for pairs of words that aren't anagrams:

```
else:

    return False
```

It's as simple as that! Now let's call our function and see if it works:

```
b = is_anagram("STAR", "RATS")

print(b)
```

You should see "True" in your console. Let's try again with two words that aren't anagrams:

```
b = is_anagram("SUN", "MOON")

print(b)
```

The answer is "False."

CODE COMPLETE!

```python
def is_anagram(word1, word2):

    if sorted(word1) == sorted(word2):

        return True

    else:

        return False


b = is_anagram("STAR", "RATS")

print(b)
```

One last thing: To a computer, uppercase and lowercase matter a lot. Keep this in mind when comparing anagrams!

YOUR TURN!

In this activity, you've practiced defining functions as well as using built-in ones. Now try adding some new features to your code!

☐ Using the *input* function, ask the user to pick two words. Don't forget to write a good prompt!

☐ Instead of printing the return value, use it in an if statement to print customized messages.

☐ Before checking if "sorted(1) == sorted(2)," add another if statement that checks if the lengths of "word1" and "word2" are equal. If not, then we already know they can't be anagrams. You can immediately return "False!"

8

The Whimsical Cupcake Shop

The Whimsical Cupcake Shop is known for its strange mishmashes of flavors. Each cupcake has two flavors: one for the cake and one for the icing. The shop is creating an "order" function to surprise their loyal customers, where the input and output look like this:

Input: How many cupcakes the customer wants (an integer)

Output: A list of cupcakes with randomly chosen surprise flavors. Each cupcake is represented with a string.

To build this function, we're going to need a for loop and the *choice* function. Let's start by importing the *choice* function from the random library! (Remember: We already did this earlier in the chapter, on page 121.) Make sure this import statement is at the top of your code file:

```
from random import choice
```

Now we define our function:

```
def order(num_cupcakes):
```

Inside the function let's create a list of flavors. This is the Whimsical Cupcake Shop, so feel free to pick flavors that are a little goofy and strange!

```
flavors = ["cherry", "mint", "bacon", "marshmallow", "peanut
butter", "zucchini", "caramel", "chocolate", "grapefruit"]
```

Choose as many or as few flavors as you want! Each cupcake is created by randomly selecting two flavors using the *choice* function. The results are stored in two variables:

```
f1 = choice(flavors)
```

```
f2 = choice(flavors)
```

The "f1" stands for "flavor 1" and "f2" stands for "flavor 2." Who knows what values are stored inside? *Choice* could have selected anything from the list of flavors—mint, grapefruit, chocolate, anything!

8

Next, we combine the two flavors into a single string. Because the chosen flavors are stored inside variables, we need to use an f-string. We'll store this new f-string inside the "cupcake" variable:

```
cupcake = f"{f1} and {f2}"
```

If you want to test out your code, you can always print the "cupcake" variable to the screen. This will let you see what value is stored inside. Delete that extra print statement when you're done testing.

If a customer orders six cupcakes, we'll need to do the random selection six times. Luckily, we have the perfect tool that makes repeating code a breeze! Put your last three lines of code inside a for loop, like this:

```
for x in range(num_cupcakes):

    f1 = choice(flavors)

    f2 = choice(flavors)

    cupcake = f"{f1} and {f2}"
```

During every round of the loop, "f1" and "f2" get new random flavors. "Cupcake" is the combination of these two flavors. On the first round, "cupcake" might be "mint and vanilla." On the second round, it might be "chocolate and cherry." We don't know, because the choices are random!

Time to store all these randomly generated cupcakes in a list. Before your for loop, we need to create an empty list to store all the cupcakes:

```
cupcake_list = []
```

It's important to define this variable outside of the for loop. Otherwise, we'll create a new "cupcake box" at each new round and all our progress will be lost.

Back inside the for loop, let's put each new cupcake inside that box:

```
cupcake_list.append(cupcake)
```

When the loop ends, we'll have a list with 4, 6, 12, or even 100 cupcakes! All that's left to do is return it:

```
return cupcake_list
```

8

And now we can call our function and test it out:

```
cupcakes = order(6)

print(cupcakes)
```

What bizarre flavor combinations did you get?

CODE COMPLETE!

```
from random import choice

def order(num_cupcakes):

    flavors = ["cherry", "mint", "bacon", "marshmallow",
    "peanut butter", "zucchini", "caramel", "chocolate",
    "grapefruit"]

    cupcake_list = []

    for x in range(num_cupcakes):

        f1 = choice(flavors)

        f2 = choice(flavors)

        cupcake = f"{f1} and {f2}"

        cupcake_list.append(cupcake)

    return cupcake_list

cupcakes = order(6)

print(cupcakes)
```

Test out your function with several different values. Have fun discovering all kinds of weird new flavors and combinations!

8

Now that you've completed this activity, are you ready for another challenge? See if you can make the following changes to this activity:

☐ Try defining the list of flavors outside your function. Then, pass it to "order" as a third parameter. What are the pros and cons of this new code?

☐ The *choice* function randomly picks a flavor. This means it's even possible to get a "chocolate and chocolate" cupcake or a "grapefruit and grapefruit" cupcake. Can you do something to prevent this? (Hint: Try removing a flavor from the list after f1 has been chosen.)

Functions Off-Screen

We need functions in programming for the same reasons that we need functions in the real world!

Think of all the people you know who have different jobs: teachers, doctors, actors, hairdressers, plumbers. Splitting up these jobs between hundreds of people allows everyone to get really good at one thing. The dentist cleans everyone's teeth. The pilot flies all the airplanes. Doing everything yourself would be exhausting!

HACKER HINTS:
TESTING YOUR FUNCTIONS

If you write a cake-baking function, you want it to bake any kind of cake. If you write a function that adds numbers, it should be able to add any numbers. To make sure your function doesn't have bugs, test it with lots of different inputs! Try big numbers, negative numbers, and zero. For strings, try testing empty strings, strings with numbers, or very long strings.

8

Giving each person a different "function" also prevents lots of mistakes. When everyone's job is clearly defined, no task gets forgotten. The world wouldn't run as smoothly if the garbage collector forgot to pick up the garbage or the radio host forgot to start their show!

Coder's Checklist

In this chapter, we covered:

☐ How functions allow us to reuse code and keep programs organized

☐ How to declare a function and its input parameters

☐ How to return values

☐ How to call a function

☐ How to use some of Python's built-in functions: *len*, *sorted*, and *choice*

☐ What libraries are and how to "borrow" functions from them

That's a lot of new stuff! Come back to this chapter anytime you want to review these lessons. Functions are a powerful coding tool, and mastering them is a key step to building cool, complex programs.

8

9

Turtle Module

A **module** is a collection of specialized functions. Functions are small blocks of code that complete a specific task, like sorting the items in a list or picking a random number.

In chapter 8, we talked about libraries and how we could "borrow" functions from them. Modules are like the sections in a library: nonfiction, mystery, fantasy, and so on. Splitting a big library into sections helps people find the books they want more quickly. It's the same idea with modules! Splitting functions into modules helps keep programmers organized.

In this chapter, we're diving into the "turtle" module. This module is full of fun, easy-to-use graphics, which will let us code *images*. Say goodbye to the console and say hello to colors, shapes, and yes, *turtles*!

Introducing the Turtle Module

You always import libraries and modules at the top of your program:

```
from turtle import *
```

The * symbol means that we're importing all the functions from the turtle module! That way, we don't have to go back and add more import statements later.

When you're using the turtle module, there are two key parts: the screen and the turtle.

The screen is your canvas. The turtle is your paintbrush (or pen). In your code, you'll use the turtle to draw shapes onto the screen. You can also use this module to make games!

When you run code from the turtle module, the screen is created automatically. You'll see a small new window pop up next to your editor and console. The turtle, on the other hand, you'll create yourself!

Objects

In the turtle module, each turtle is an object. An **object** is a user-defined data structure. We use objects to keep related variables and functions in the same place. Instead of needing 10 or 20 different variables, we can store them all in a single object. Much more organized!

An object's variables are called **attributes**. A turtle object, for example, will have attributes that define its shape, size, and color.

Objects also have special functions called **methods**. Methods define what an object is meant to do. The turtle object, for example, can move around the canvas, draw shapes, change colors, move fast or slow, etc.

This book won't show you how to define your own objects, but you'll get plenty of practice using the objects, attributes, and methods of the turtle module. If you want to explore this subject more, check out the Resources section (page 180) for fun coding websites, magazines, and more!

9

Making Your Turtle

Now that we've imported the module, we can create our turtle. Make sure you write "Turtle" with a capital "T," and don't forget the round brackets!

```
shelly = Turtle()
```

The code "Turtle()" creates a new turtle object, which we store in the variable named "shelly," just like going to a virtual pet store, adopting a turtle, and naming her "Shelly!"

A turtle object comes with all kinds of built-in attributes and methods. In other words, Shelly already knows how to do things like move around and change colors. We don't have to teach her. Later on, when we want to use these attributes and methods, we'll use the "shelly" variable to access the turtle object.

Run the code in your editor. A small window should pop up, with a tiny triangle in the middle.

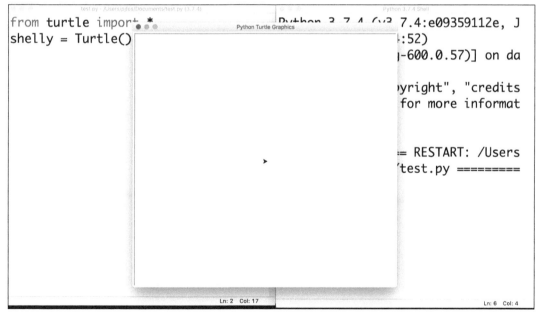

That tiny triangle is our turtle, Shelly! But she doesn't really look like a turtle yet, does she? Let's use the *shape* method to change that:

```
shelly.shape("turtle")
```

To use an object's method:

- Start with the variable that stores the object (in this case, it's "shelly").

- Add a period (.).

- Write the name of the method, followed by round brackets. Just like a regular function!

- If the function needs parameters, write your values in between the brackets. Remember, parameters are special variables used to collect function input. We covered them in chapter 8 (page 113)!

Does the syntax look a little familiar? We've used it before, in chapter 5 (page 57)! In Python, lists are a type of object, and *append* and *remove* are object methods.

To use the *shape* method, you need to pass an argument (value) to the function. This argument is a string and it tells the method what kind of shape we want: a triangle, a circle, or in this case, a turtle!

If you run your code, you should see a tiny turtle on your screen:

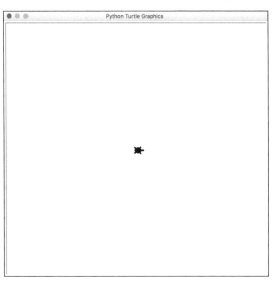

There she is! What a good turtle.

Making the Turtle Move

Let's make Shelly move! The simplest choice is the *forward* method:

```
shelly.forward(100)
```

The *forward* method needs one argument: an integer, which represents how many pixels (a tiny unit of length) you want Shelly to move forward. Try the code out!

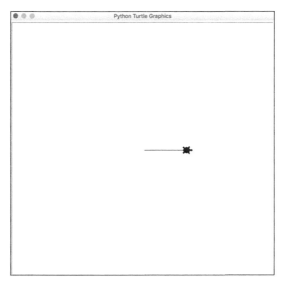

See how Shelly darted forward, drawing a line as she went? It's a pretty small line—remember, pixels aren't very big! You can also move Shelly backwards using the *backward* method:

```
shelly.backward(100)
```

Now, Shelly has returned to her starting point! Both *forward* and *backward* depend on the direction that Shelly is facing. By default, the turtle starts looking to the right, but we can change that using the *right* and *left* methods.

Right needs one number as an argument, which represents an angle. So if we want Shelly to turn 90 degrees to the right, we'd write:

```
shelly.right(90)
```

Now, Shelly is facing the bottom of the screen! What happens if we make her move forward again? (Psst: Either write the next block of code in a new editor or delete your previous lines of code. Otherwise, your results will be wonky!)

```
shelly.forward(100)

shelly.right(90)

shelly.forward(100)
```

This code makes Shelly moves 100 paces forward, turn 90 degrees to the right to face the bottom, and move another 100 paces forward:

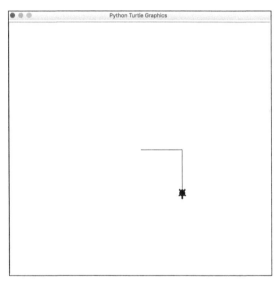

The *left* function is the same as right, except that Shelly turns in the opposite direction. Let's have Shelly draw a square. Overall, the code to move the turtle should look like this:

```
shelly.forward(100)

shelly.left(90)

shelly.forward(100)

shelly.left(90)
```

9

```
shelly.forward(100)

shelly.left(90)

shelly.forward(100)
```

We call the *forward* function four times, to make four sides. In between each one, Shelly turns 90 degrees to the left, to face a new direction. The result is a perfect square!

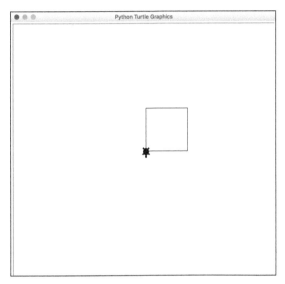

There's one more interesting function that gets Shelly moving. *Forward* and *backward* make straight lines and are perfect for drawing shapes like squares, rectangles, triangles, and octagons. But if you want to draw a circle, then you want the *circle* function. This method also takes one argument:

```
shelly.circle(100)
```

The number inside the brackets represents the radius of the circle. The radius is the distance from the edge of circle to the center. So a small radius means a small circle, and a big radius means a big circle. Let's try it out!

```
shelly.circle(20)

shelly.circle(250)
```

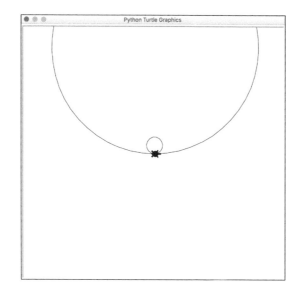

You can make Shelly draw a circle anywhere on the screen. Between *forward*, *backward*, *left*, *right*, and *circle*, there are so many images you can create!

9

Changing Colors

Ready to take your artistic masterpieces to the next level? To change the color of your paintbrush (or pen), use the *pencolor* method. Then, let's make Shelly go in a circle:

```
shelly.pencolor("blue")

shelly.circle(100)
```

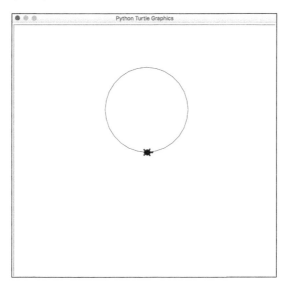

Pencolor needs one string as an argument. This string should be a color, such as blue, green, red, yellow, orange, or pink. Make sure to spell it with lowercase letters. And since *pencolor* is a method, we have to call it using a turtle object. If you just wrote "pencolor("blue")," the code wouldn't work. Just like *forward*, *backward*, and *circle*—all methods must be attached to an object!

Shelly can only use colors that are built into the turtle library. Luckily, there are lots! You can get wild with really specific shades like "dark orchid" and "medium spring green." You can find the full list of built-in colors here: tcl.tk/man/tcl8.6 /TkCmd/colors.htm.

9

To make things even more colorful, we can fill in the shapes that Shelly has drawn and create even better pictures. To begin, we use the *fillcolor* method to pick the color that will fill the shapes. This method is similar to *pencolor*: it takes one string argument and that string must be a color.

Then, we call the *begin_fill* and *end_fill* methods. Neither of these functions have parameters. When writing your code, you start with a call to *begin_fill*, then you draw your shape, and finally you end with *end_fill*. The code looks like this:

```
shelly.fillcolor("purple")

shelly.begin_fill()

shelly.circle(100)

shelly.end_fill()
```

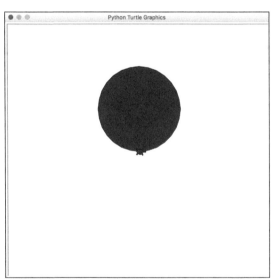

You can draw any shape you want—triangles, squares, hexagons. Instead of calling the *circle* method in between *begin_fill* and *end_fill*, use a combination of *forward* and *right* to create any of these new shapes.

Finally, we can make our canvas prettier by changing the background color of the screen. This *bgcolor* function is a little different. For starters, it's not a method. You can call it with no object:

```
bgcolor("light green")
```

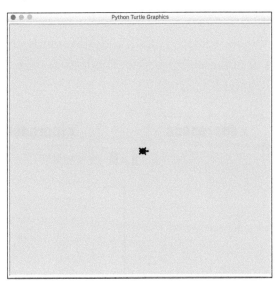

Look at that happy little turtle! Like the methods we've seen in the turtle module, *bgcolor* needs one string argument. Between *pencolor*, *fillcolor*, and *bgcolor*, you can create some beautiful designs on your canvas!

Working with Screen Coordinates

Understanding how to use the screen's coordinate system will let us move our turtle to specific places. This means we can draw prettier, more detailed pictures!

When you use the turtle module, the program creates a new, separate window where your turtles can zoom around. The window is separated into four areas. Picture two lines, one horizontal and one vertical, dividing the screen down and across the middle.

9

These lines are your x-axis and y-axis. The center, where they meet, is position (0, 0). When we write coordinates, we always write the x-coordinate first, followed by the y-coordinate.

If Shelly travels to the right, her x-coordinate increases. If she goes left, the x-coordinate decreases. If she goes up, the y-coordinate increases, and if she goes down, the y-coordinate decreases.

You can visualize the coordinate system with this handy chart. The screen is designed as a square of 600 pixels per side. The four corners are (-300, -300), (-300, 300), (300, 300), and (300, -300).

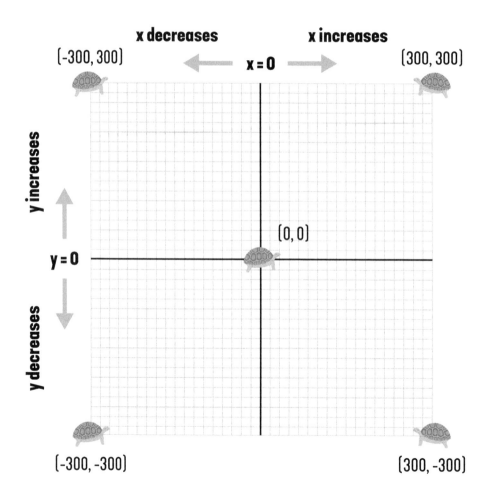

To make Shelly go to a point on the screen, we can use the *goto* function. *Goto* has two parameters: an x-coordinate and a y-coordinate.

```
shelly.goto(100, 100)
```

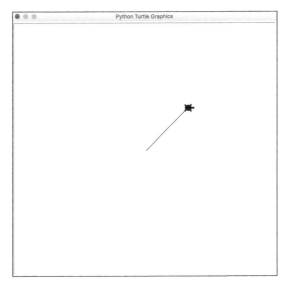

See how Shelly draws a diagonal line that goes up and right? That's because we gave her a positive x-coordinate and a positive y-coordinate. Try sending Shelly to different positions. Don't forget to try coordinates with negative numbers!

HACKER HINTS:
USING THE CONSOLE FOR DEBUGGING

When you run your turtle code, a new screen pops up. However, you can still print values to your console. This is really useful if you've got a bug in your code, because printing variables can help you find it. Switch back and forth between the two screens to see what's going on.

9

Go, Turtle, Go! (Turtle Module in Action)

The turtle library is perfect for creating games or drawing beautiful pictures. Let's build a few together and combine our old coding tools with these new ones. Remember to code your activities in the editor, not the shell!

Spiraling Out of Control!

LEVEL UP!

Shelly's been drawing so many circles that she's made herself dizzy. She's spiraling out of control!

We know how to make a turtle draw a circle, but what about a *spiral*? Using an extra variable and a for loop, let's create this new shape.

As always, we need to import the turtle library:

```
from turtle import *
```

Next, we create our turtle:

```
shelly = Turtle()
```

If you want, you can also change Shelly's shape using the *shape* function. Remember, the method takes one argument—a string!

```
shelly.shape("turtle")
```

We've seen how to call the *circle* method with one parameter. There's also a version with two parameters. The first parameter is still the radius of the circle, but the second parameter is an angle. If you put "360," Shelly will draw a full circle:

```
shelly.circle(50, 360)
```

But if you put "180," Shelly only draws half a circle. Try out these two lines of code, then delete them when you're done:

```
shelly.circle(50, 180)
```

9

To create our spiral, we'll start with a half-circle. Then, we'll draw another half-circle, but slightly bigger. Then a third, slightly bigger again. This creates the spiral effect!

To make this work, let's store the length of the radius in a variable.

```python
radius = 50
```

Next, since we're drawing half-circles over and over, it's time for a for loop! Let's start with 10 rounds:

```python
for counter in range(10):

    shelly.circle(radius, 180)
```

In the first line of this code block, we define our for loop. The *range* function decides the number of rounds, and we're passing it a "10."

To draw the circle, we use the *circle* method with two parameters. On the first round, the "radius" value stores the value "50." That'll be the size of the circle. The second parameter is set to 180 degrees, so we only draw a half-circle.

At each round of the loop, we want the half-circle to be slightly bigger. So after drawing a half-circle, let's increase the "radius" variable:

```python
radius += 20
```

Make sure you're increasing the radius inside the for loop, so it gets bigger every round!

CODE COMPLETE!

```python
from turtle import *


shelly = Turtle()

shelly.shape("turtle")

radius = 50
```

9

```
for counter in range(10):

    shelly.circle(radius, 180)

    radius += 20
```

Shelly should look something like this:

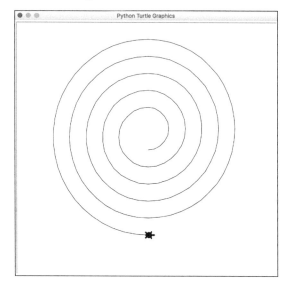

Try out your code and watch Shelly keep on spinning. That's one dizzy little turtle!

YOUR TURN!

We've practiced using the circle method in a new, fun way. How can you make the code better?

☐ Try tweaking some of the numbers in your code. Instead of a radius of 50, start at 100. Instead of adding 20 at each lap, try multiplying "radius" by 1.3.

☐ Add a background color to your canvas and add some color to the spiral!

☐ Can you make Shelly draw a spiral in reverse? She should end up back where she started.

Bungee Jump!

Shelly is going bungee jumping! Using a for loop and the *forward* and *backward* functions, let's animate our little turtle's adventures.

Start by importing the turtle library:

```
from turtle import *
```

Then, create Shelly and give her a turtle shape:

```
shelly = Turtle()

shelly.shape("turtle")
```

Next, let's make the animation more fun to watch! If we slow down Shelly using the *speed* method, her bungee jumping won't look so wild:

```
shelly.speed("slowest")
```

The *speed* method takes one string as an argument. You can choose options like "normal," "fast," or "slow."

Time for the bungee jumping! Right now, Shelly is still staring at the right side of the screen. To make her look at the bottom of the screen, we need to turn her to the right by 90 degrees:

```
shelly.right(90)
```

Finally, let's choose a length for the bungee-jumping cord. This value will decide how far down she goes:

```
cord_length = 150
```

Let's say that Shelly gets five rounds of bungee jumping in one session. Since all the rounds are pretty similar, we can use a for loop to repeat them:

```
for counter in range(5):
```

9

At the start of the first round, Shelly jumps off the platform. Since she's facing downward, we can use the *forward* function. The distance is determined by the length of the bungee-jumping cord:

```
shelly.forward(cord_length)
```

Once she reaches the bottom, the cord pulls her back up! However, because she's moving so fast, it's going to pull her back up slightly farther than the starting platform. We can add this into our code by multiplying "cord_length" by 1.1 inside the round brackets:

```
shelly.backward(cord_length * 1.1)
```

If *forward* brings Shelly down, then *backward* will bring her back up. If the value of "cord_length" is "150," then "cord_length * 1.1" will be 165. Shelly will be 15 pixels above her starting platform.

Since Shelly is now starting higher up, she has more momentum, and she's going to fall a little farther. Let's increase the "cord_length" variable inside our for loop:

```
cord_length += 50
```

On the second round, Shelly will fall 200 feet. On the third round, it'll be 250.

CODE COMPLETE!

```
from turtle import *


shelly = Turtle()

shelly.shape("turtle")

shelly.speed("slowest")

shelly.right(90)
```

```
cord_length = 150


for counter in range(5):

    shelly.forward(cord_length)

    shelly.backward(cord_length * 1.1)

    cord_length += 50
```

Double-check your indentation and run your code. Have fun watching Shelly bob up and down—what an adventurous little turtle!

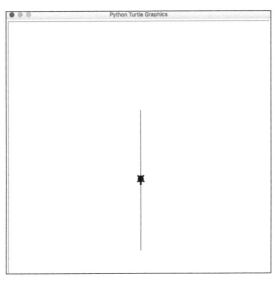

YOUR TURN!

Shelly is having the time of her life bungee jumping, thanks to you! Can you add even more cool features to the program?

☐ When Shelly's facing the right, *forward* brings her to the right and *backward* brings her to the left. Before she starts bungee jumping, have Shelly draw a starting platform using these methods.

☐ Can you make Shelly's speed increase every couple of rounds? From "slowest," you could change her speed to "slow," then "normal," then "fast." (Hint: Use the counter variable of the for loop to figure out what round it is, then use an if statement.)

Very Curious Turtles

LEVEL UP!

Shelly and her friend Sheldon want to explore a park. They've packed their bags with snacks, sunscreen, and water bottles, and they're ready to explore every inch of greenery!

Using a while loop, the *goto* function, and the random library, let's write some code that'll help them explore.

To start, we need to import two libraries:

```
from turtle import *

from random import randint
```

We're importing everything from the turtle module, but we're only borrowing one function from the random library: *randint. Randint* is a function that creates random integers. Later, we'll use it to create coordinates and decide where Shelly and Sheldon explore!

Now, let's create Shelly and Sheldon:

```
shelly = Turtle()

sheldon = Turtle()
```

To tell the two turtles apart, let's give them each a different color using the *pencolor* function. You can choose your own colors for the turtles or copy the ones here:

```
shelly.pencolor("purple")

sheldon.pencolor("green")
```

Now, let's change the background color of the screen. This will make the park more exciting for Shelly and Sheldon to explore:

```
bgcolor("light green")
```

Since *bgcolor* isn't a method, we don't need to call it with an object. You're also free to choose any color you want: green, dark green, light blue, pink, or even yellow!

To keep our code simple, we're going to do something that's usually forbidden: We're going to use an infinite while loop!

```
while True:
```

The condition of this while loop is "True." "True" is always True! And since our condition depends on a value, not a variable, it can't be changed.

This means you'll have to stop your program manually, either by closing the window or pressing CTRL+C, but it also means Shelly and Sheldon can wander as long as they like, inspecting flowers, insects, and birds.

Now, it's time to choose the exact locations that Shelly and Sheldon will explore. Remember how every point on the screen can be found using an x-coordinate and a y-coordinate? We'll use the *randint* function to choose these coordinates randomly:

```
shelly_x = randint(-300, 300)
```

The *randint* function takes two arguments. The first is the smallest value that the function is allowed to choose. The second argument is the biggest value. Both parameters must be integers. In this example, *randint* chooses a number between -300 and 300 and stores it in the "shelly_x" variable.

Why did we choose "-300" and "300" as the parameters? Remember, the four corners of the screen are (-300, -300), (-300, 300), (300, 300), and (300, -300). If you choose a number higher than 300 or lower than -300, Shelly will leave the screen completely!

Let's choose random numbers three more times, for the other coordinates!

9

```
shelly_y = randint(-300, 300)

sheldon_x = randint(-300, 300)

sheldon_y = randint(-300, 300)
```

We've created four random integers, two for Shelly and two for Sheldon. The variables "shelly_x" and "shelly_y" will store the x-coordinates and y-coordinates for Shelly. So, if "shelly_x" is "45" and "shelly_y" is "120," then Shelly will head to position (45, 120).

Next, we use the *goto* function to send Shelly and Sheldon to these new positions:

```
shelly.goto(shelly_x, shelly_y)

sheldon.goto(sheldon_x, sheldon_y)
```

Make sure that "shelly_x" and "shelly_y" are matched with Shelly, and "sheldon_x" and "sheldon_y" with Sheldon!

Each round of the while loop, we create four new random numbers, then we send Shelly and Sheldon to explore these new positions. If you run your code, you'll see the two turtles bounce around the screen, exploring every inch of their new park!

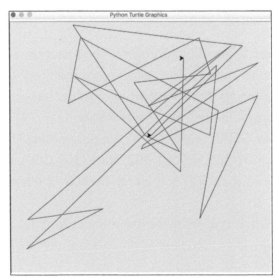

Because you're using an infinite while loop, you have to stop the program manually. There are three ways to do this in IDLE:

- Close the window using the "X" in the top corner.

- Hit CTRL+C.

- Click on "Shell" at the top of the screen and then select "Restart Shell."

CODE COMPLETE!

```python
from turtle import *

from random import randint


shelly = Turtle()

sheldon = Turtle()

shelly.pencolor("purple")

sheldon.pencolor("green")


bgcolor("light green")


while True:

    shelly_x = randint(-300, 300)

    shelly_y = randint(-300, 300)

    sheldon_x = randint(-300, 300)

    sheldon_y = randint(-300, 300)

    shelly.goto(shelly_x, shelly_y)

    sheldon.goto(sheldon_x, sheldon_y)
```

9

Run your code and watch Shelly and Sheldon explore! See how the turtles randomly move to new coordinates?

YOUR TURN!

Shelly and Sheldon are having a blast exploring their new park that you created for them. Now, let's make their adventure even more exciting!

☐ Try drawing some interesting shapes at different coordinates for Shelly and Sheldon to go visit.

☐ Play with methods like *shape* and *speed* to change how the program looks.

☐ Create a few more friends for Shelly and Sheldon and place all these Turtle objects in a list. To generate new coordinates for each turtle, make them "goto" a new position. (Hint: Use a for each loop inside the while loop when creating these new numbers and telling each turtle where to go).

Modules Off-Screen

Modules aren't just a programming concept—they pop up in the real world, too! Look around all the stuff in your house. If you put it all into a big pile, it'd probably be hard to find things. In order to stay organized, you separate stuff into different rooms: knives and forks go in the kitchen, bicycles go in the garage, clothes go in your bedroom closet.

Separating functions into different modules is just like separating objects into different rooms. When we want to build a website, we know we'll find the right functions in the web module. When we want to build multimedia games with cool images, we'll look in the graphics modules.

Modules are also useful for a second reason: They let us import only the functions we need! When you go to school, you don't bring *all* your possessions with you. That'd be way too heavy and it wouldn't fit in your backpack! The same thing applies to code. If we didn't split all that code into modules, it would slow our programs down. With modules, we can pick and choose what we need.

9

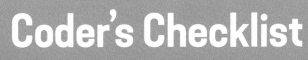

Coder's Checklist

In the chapter, you learned:

☐ What modules are and how to import them

☐ What objects are

☐ How to create a Turtle object and store it in a variable

☐ How to make Turtles move

☐ How to use colors with the Turtle module

☐ How the screen can be separated into coordinates

Turtle is a really fun module for drawing pictures and creating games. Now that you know the basics, see where your imagination takes you! You can go over the sections of this chapter whenever you want to jog your memory.

9

10

Game On: Putting It All Together

You've learned about variables, data types, data structures, conditionals, loops, and functions. Now it's time to have some fun and challenge yourself even more! Building a game is a great way to practice coding. By the end, you'll have an even better understanding of all your new coding tools, and you can combine them to solve complicated problems and build your own games from scratch!

Ready to put your skills to the test?

Rules of the Game

We're going to create a space-themed version of "Code Breaker" called "Spaceships and Aliens."

Picture a not-so-distant future where humans live all across the galaxy. You, a spaceship captain, have intercepted a secret message from another ship. To decode the message, you need to crack a 4-digit code.

Your codebreaking software can tell if you've guessed the *right* digit at the *right* position, which we'll call a *spaceship*. It'll also tell you if you've guessed the *right* digit at the *wrong* position, which we'll call an *alien*. Digits that aren't spaceships or aliens get ignored.

For example: Let's say the code is "7832," and your guess is "7628."

- Both your guess and the code start with a 7. Right digit, right position. That's one spaceship!

- Both your guess and the code have an "8" and a "2." However, the "8" is the second digit of the code, and the fourth digit of the guess. There's a similar problem with the "2": right digit, but the wrong position. That's two aliens!

- So the result of this guess would be "1S2A": one spaceship and two aliens.

One other thing: When choosing codes, we have to make sure that all four digits are different. Otherwise, the game won't work!

Bite by Byte: Building Your Game

When you build a big program, you don't want to write *all* the code at once. Instead, we want to think logically, like a programmer, and start with a small piece. We run our code, test it, and fix any bugs, then we can move on to the next piece. This makes code easier to debug, and it also stops us from "biting off more than we can chew!"

Comments: For Your Eyes Only

Big programs can have thousands of lines of code. To stay organized, programmers use comments to describe what a section of code is doing. **Comments** are lines of text that are ignored by the program. They're for human eyes only!

In Python, there are two ways to write comments.

1. There's the short, one-line comment:

```
# A secret message has been intercepted!
```

Start the line with the "#" symbol. When the program runs, that entire line will be skipped! You can also add comments halfway through a line:

```
message = "2HFHOUWAHIFGA" # this message is gibberish
```

Everything to the right of the "#" symbol is ignored.

2. There's also the multiline comment:

```
""" This function decodes a secret message

Input: the secret message (a string)

Output: a Boolean value """
```

Use three quotation marks (""") to start your comment, and three more to end it.

Good variable names make code easier to read, but sometimes we need a little more help to understand what's going on. Comments help with this. You might want to start functions, for example, with a comment that explains what their task is.

Comments are especially helpful when you haven't looked at your code in months or if someone else is trying to understand the logic of your code!

Let's Code!

To start, we'll print some instructions to the screen and set up our game. Then, we'll create a secret code for you, the player, to crack! In our version, the game ends when you've correctly guessed all four digits.

3, 2, 1—Liftoff!: Starting Your Game

To begin, let's tell the user what game they're playing:

```
print("Welcome to Spaceships and Aliens!")
```

We also want to explain the instructions:

```
print("Your goal is to crack a secret 4-digit code. All the
digits in the code are unique!")
```

```
print("A spaceship (S) means you've guessed the right digit
at the right position.")
```

```
print("An alien (A) means you've guessed the right digit, but
at the wrong position!")
```

```
print("Wrong digits get ignored.")
```

The game is in full swing! Now, it's time to create our 4-digit secret code. Using the *input* function, let's ask the user to pick something and type it into the console. The text prompt should mention that all the digits need to be unique!

```
secret_code = input("Pick a secret code with 4 different
digits: ")
```

If you want to play the game yourself, get a friend or family member to type in the secret code. No peeking!

Next, we need to hide this secret code from the user. If we just leave it in the console, the user won't have to guess–the code will be right in front of them!

10

To hide the secret code, let's print 100 blank lines. This will replace the text in the console and hide the secret code. Since we're repeating code, let's use a for loop:

```
for counter in range(100):

    print()
```

We don't need to put any text inside the *print* function because we're not trying to display a message. We just want blank lines! And since our *range* function has the value "100," we know that the *print* function will run 100 times, giving us 100 blank lines in total.

Now the user can enter their first guess. They probably *won't* guess the correct code on their first try. They might need 10 tries, or 100! Since we don't know the number of guesses they'll need, we should use a while loop.

First, let's create a "guess" variable with a **dummy value**:

```
guess = "0000"
```

Since the secret code is a 4-digit string, then the user's guess should be a 4-digit string as well. But we also know that the secret code can't actually be "0000," because the code will have four different digits! We're just giving "guess" a dummy value to get the loop started.

The game ends when the user guesses the secret code. This means the game continues as long as "guess" and "secret_code" don't match!

```
while secret_code != guess:
```

The expression "secret_code != guess" is True when the variables have *different* values. That means our loop will only run while the user makes *incorrect* guesses!

Inside the loop, we ask the user for a guess. Don't forget to write a good prompt in your *input* function!

```
guess = input("Enter a 4-digit code: ")
```

Remember, *input* functions always return strings. Whatever the user types into the console will be stored in the variable "guess" as a string.

So far, your code for the game should look like this:

```python
print("Welcome to Spaceships and Aliens!")


print("Your goal is to crack a secret 4-digit code. All the
digits in the code are unique!")

print("A spaceship (S) means you've guessed the right digit
at the right position.")

print("An alien (A) means you've guessed the right digit, but
at the wrong position!")

print("Wrong digits get ignored.")


secret_code = input("Pick a secret code with 4 different
digits: ")

for counter in range(100):

    print()

guess = "0000"


while secret_code != guess:

    guess = input("Enter a 4-digit code: ")
```

Win or Lose? Comparing the Guess and the Secret Code

It's time to see if the user has cracked the secret code! Comparing the user's guess to the secret code isn't a simple task. Are the right digits in the right positions? Or does the guess have the right digits, but in the wrong order?

Since this is a task we'll repeat often, let's put the code inside another function called "compare_guess."

The input of this function has two parameters: the secret code and the player's guess.

The output is a string that tells us about the player's guess. How many spaceships were in the guess? How many aliens?

You should write your "compare_guess" function at the top of your file, before the first print statement. In general, you should structure the program inside your editor like this:

1. Import statements

2. Function definitions

3. All the other code

We write code in this order because you can't call a function that hasn't been defined, and you can't use a library that hasn't been imported!

Next, since the "compare_guess" function needs two parameters, let's separate them with a comma in between the round brackets. Let's also add a comment above the function to describe exactly what it does, to make sure our code is clearly labeled:

```
# Compares the player's guess to the secret code by looking
at each digit, one at a time

def compare_guess(secret_code, guess):
```

The goal of this function is to see how many spaceships and aliens are in the user's guess. Let's create variables to store these numbers. Don't forget to indent all the code inside your function!

```
    num_spaceships = 0

    num_aliens = 0
```

The values start at 0, because we haven't checked any digits yet. Whenever two digits match, we'll increase either "num_spaceships" or "num_aliens" by 1. Since we want to check each digit, one at a time, we can use a for loop:

```
for i in range(4):
```

"Range(4)" means the loop will have four rounds—one for each digit. The "i" is our counter variable that stores the index of the digit we're checking. On the first round of the loop, the value of "i" will be "0." On the second round, it'll be "1," then "2," and finally "3."

Since both "secret_code" and "guess" are strings, we can treat them like lists and access digits using their indices. Let's say that "secret_code" is 5682 and the "guess" is 5204. To check if the two first digits match, we'd write:

```
secret_code[0] == guess[0]
```

In this case, the Boolean expression would be True, because the first digit of both lists is "5." However, we eventually want to check all four digits. So instead of "0," let's use "i". Remember, the value of "i" is always changing! This lets us check each digit one at a time.

If the digits of both codes match, we increase our "num_spaceships" variable:

```
for i in range(4):

    if guess[i] == secret_code[i]:

        num_spaceships += 1
```

Take a look at this code—on the first round of the loop, when "i" is 0, we're checking the two digits at index 0. On the next round, we check the two digits at index 1, and so on. If none of the digits match, we'll end the loop with zero spaceships. And if all the digits match, we'll have four spaceships and we'll win the game!

The next step is to check for aliens—digits that match but aren't at the same position. To check if a digit is somewhere in a list (or string), we can use the "in" keyword. For example, if we write:

```
5 in secret_code
```

The expression is True if the number 5 is one of the digits in "secret_code." It could be the first digit, or the second, or the last—doesn't matter! It just has to be there. If none of the digits are 5, then the whole expression is False.

10

Since we're checking for spaceships with the first branch of our conditional, we'll use a second branch—an elif—to check for aliens:

```
elif guess[i] in secret_code:

    num_aliens += 1
```

Let's review what we've done with this function:

1. We used a for loop to check each digit, one at a time.

2. Starting at index 0, we checked if the first two digits of "secret_code" and "guess" were equal using the equals-to operator (==).

3. If the digits matched, great! We increased "num_spaceships" and skipped the rest of the conditional.

4. But if the digits didn't match, we checked the elif. Even though the guessed digit ("guess[i]") wasn't at the right position, we checked if the digit might still be somewhere *else* in the list. If it was, that means we found an alien, and we increased "num_aliens."

5. The for loop increased the value of "i" to 1. Next, we checked the digits at index 1.

6. We repeated steps 2 through 5 until all the digits were checked.

By the end of the for loop, we've found all the spaceships and aliens in the user's guess. The next step in our game is to tell the user the results of their guess!

We want our output to be a string with a format that might look like "2S0A" or "1S1A," depending on which digits matched. Remember, the "S" stands for spaceships and the "A" for aliens.

Using an f-string, we can combine text and variables:

```
result = f"{num_spaceships}S{num_aliens}A"
```

Finish the function by returning this variable:

```
return result
```

The function is done! Your code for the function should look like this—make sure the indentation lines up properly in your editor:

```python
# Compares the player's guess to the secret code by looking
at each digit, one at a time

def compare_guess(secret_code, guess):

    num_spaceships = 0

    num_aliens = 0

    for i in range(4):

        if guess[i] == secret_code[i]:

            num_spaceships += 1

        elif guess[i] in secret_code:

            num_aliens += 1

    result = f"{num_spaceships}S{num_aliens}A"

    return result
```

Now we can compare the user's guess with the secret code anytime we want!

Testing Your Code

Before we move on to the next step, let's make sure the function works by testing it! Since this code is just used for testing, you can delete it when you're done.

To start, let's create dummy variables with good test values:

```python
test_code = [1, 2, 3, 4]

test_guess = [1, 2, 3, 4]
```

As you can see, the digits of "test_code" and "test_guess" are identical. That's because we want our function to find four spaceships and zero aliens. Let's see what happens when we call the function:

```
test_result = compare_guess(test_code, test_guess)
```

Make sure that "test_code" is the first argument so it matches the parameters in our function definition. Then, print the result to the console:

```
print(test_result)
```

Did you get the right answer? If your "compare_guess" function works properly, you should see "4S0A" in your console–four spaceships and zero aliens!

Tweak the values of "test_code" and "test_guess" for another couple tests. What if we want to test values that will give us a result of zero spaceships and four aliens? Or two spaceships and two aliens–or even a case with zero spaceships and zero aliens? Try coming up with your own values, and give them a quick test.

Everything looking good? Great! Now delete your test code and get ready to finish the game!

Are We There Yet?: Finishing the Game

Almost finished!

For the next step, let's go back to our while loop:

```
while secret_code != guess:

    guess = ("Enter a 4-digit code: ")
```

You now have the function you need to compare the user's guess with the secret code. Let's call "compare_guess" and store the result in a new variable. Make sure you match the order of the parameters!

```
result = compare_guess(secret_code, guess)
```

How do we know if the user won the game?

If all the digits of "guess" are correct and in the correct positions, the "compare_guess" function will find four spaceships and zero aliens. That means the value stored in "result" will be "4S0A." Let's check that!

If this Boolean expression is True, then we can congratulate our player!

```
if result == "4S0A":

    print("Congratulations! You broke the secret code!")
```

But if the player hasn't won yet, let's pass along the result of their guess:

```
else:

    print(result)
```

If the result is something like "2S1A"–two spaceships and one alien–that string will be printed to the console. It's an important clue for the player that'll help them decide what to guess next.

That's it for the main code! Once the player has won, the values in "guess" and "secret_code" will be identical. The condition of our while loop is only True when these two variables are different. If they're the same, then the while loop ends automatically.

Don't forget to double-check your code for typos, mistakes with indentation, and forgotten brackets!

CODE COMPLETE!

```
# Compares the player's guess to the secret code by looking
at each digit, one at a time

def compare_guess(secret_code, guess):

    num_spaceships = 0

    num_aliens = 0

    for i in range(4):

        if guess[i] == secret_code[i]:

            num_spaceships += 1

        elif guess[i] in secret_code:

            num_aliens += 1
```

```python
    result = f"{num_spaceships}S{num_aliens}A"

    return result

print("Welcome to Spaceships and Aliens!")

print("Your goal is to crack a secret 4-digit code. All the
digits in the code are unique!")

print("A spaceship(S) means you've guessed the right digit at
the right position.")

print("An alien (A) means you've guessed the right digit, but
at the wrong position!")

print("Wrong digits get ignored.")

secret_code = input("Pick a secret code with 4 different
digits: ")

for counter in range(100):

    print()

guess = "0000"

while secret_code != guess:

    guess = input("Enter a 4-digit code: ")

    result = compare_guess(secret_code, guess)

    if result == "4S0A":

        print("Congratulations! You broke the secret code!")

    else:

        print(result)
```

Congratulations—you've built an entire game with Python code!

When you're ready, run your game and see how long it takes you to crack the code. Once you've worked out any bugs in your game, challenge friends and family members!

Taking "Spaceships and Aliens" to the Next Level

"Spaceships and Aliens" is just *one* example of the fun games and programs you can build in Python. There are lots of features you can add to make your game even better! Try adding one (or more!) of these ideas to your game for the ultimate challenge.

Bring a Friend!

Cracking secret codes is fun, but it's even more fun when you're playing against a friend!

If you want to add a second player, you'll have to create a second secret code. Luckily, you can call the "create_secret_code" function as many times as you want:

```
secret_code2 = input("Pick another secret code with
4 different digits: ")
```

You're also going to need a new variable for Player 2's guess:

```
guess1 = "0000"
```

```
guess2 = "0000"
```

Since there's only one console, Player 1 and Player 2 will have to guess one at a time. What coding structures should you repeat inside your while loop to make this work?

Beat the Clock!

To make the game harder, limit the number of guesses each player is allowed.

To start, you'll need a variable that keeps track of guesses. This should be defined before the while loop:

```
guesses_left = 25
```

Whenever the user doesn't guess correctly, remove one guess. You can put this in your else statement:

```
guesses_left -= 1
```

What other changes should you make? You'll probably need to modify the condition of your while loop. (Hint: "guesses_left" should always be greater than 0!)

The Finishing Touches

Here are a few more ideas you can add to your game:

- Use a dictionary to keep track of all the guesses a player has made and the results of those guesses.

- Add a funny print statement that tells the user how good their guess was. You can use a conditional to customize these messages.

- Add a special "hint" feature, where the user can unlock one digit of the secret code.

Feel free to come up with your own ideas! You have all the fundamental coding tools you need to make any change you want.

In this chapter, you built a game using functions, a while loop, for loops, conditionals, and lists. You used the *print* and *input* functions to make your game interactive. That's a lot of tools! Best of all, you've learned how to tackle problems by thinking like a programmer.

Give yourself a high-five—you've earned it!

10

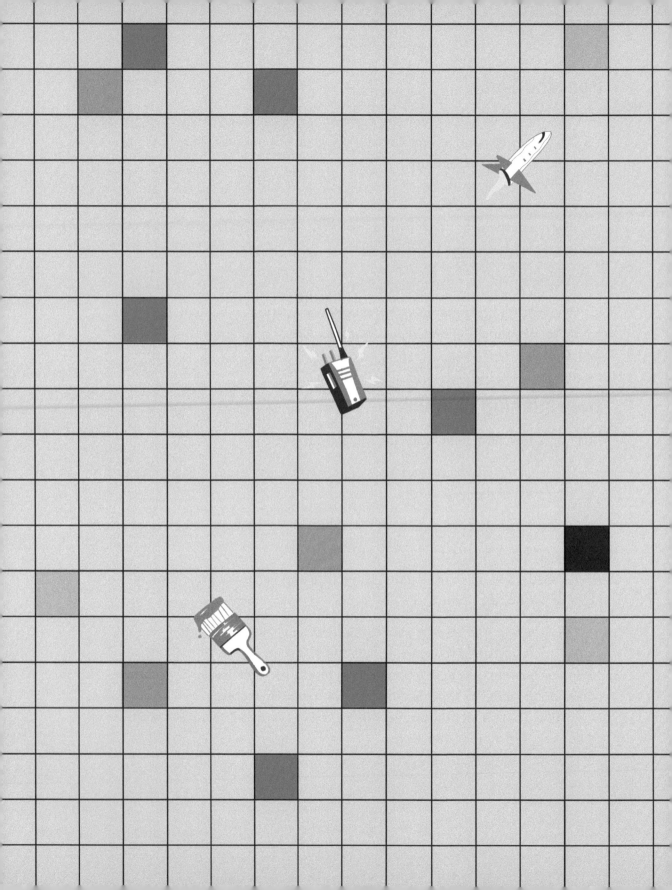

Code for the Road

Congratulations—you did it! You've reached the end of your first coding adventure. Give yourself a pat on the back and look at how far you've come.

You built over 20 programs using variables, data structures, conditionals, loops, and functions. You created a big, interactive game and learned how to debug. And best of all, you learned how different coding tools can solve different problems. Whenever you run into a new challenge, think about your toolbox. Can the problem be solved with repetition? By splitting it into different tasks? By changing a condition?

It's okay if you're still getting stuck on certain concepts. Like anything, coding takes practice! You're learning a whole new language—Python—and all those terms and rules take time to master. Keep going through the different lessons, especially those you found tricky. By practicing coding again and again, it'll become easier and more natural, and soon you'll find yourself looking for bigger challenges! Maybe you'll even use your new Python skills to help you bring your own programs and games to life!

Thinking like a programmer is about breaking down a complicated problem into small pieces. That's a skill that can help you in the real world! Whenever you're faced with a big project, like a camping trip, an essay, or an art project, try tackling it like a programmer—one step at a time.

One of the fun things about coding is that the basics stay the same, no matter what language you use. Another cool thing about coding is that there's always more to learn. More languages, more libraries, more algorithms. If you're ready to keep going, check out the **Resources** section (page 180) for great websites and more.

Happy coding!

Bug Hunting: Troubleshooting Tips

Your program crashed, or it's not quite working how you want. Looks like you've got a bug to find!

Whether you're a beginner or you've been coding for years, the first draft of any program is almost never perfect. The key is to hunt for bugs in a calm, logical order. If you need a break, go ahead and take one! Sometimes, just leaving the computer and coming back later can clear your head and make a bug easier to find.

But if you're hungry to find that bug, here's where to start:

1. If your program crashed, first look at the error in your console.

    In all that red text, you'll see a line number. Maybe "line 2" or "line 27." This is the line of code where the crash happened. Then, you can go find it in your editor. This is the best place to start your bug hunt.

2. Next, check your code for spelling mistakes.

    Typos happen to every programmer! Here are some of the most common typing errors:

    *   Misspelling a variable name. You named your variable "unicorn," but later on you typed "unicrn." You'll get a "NameError" in the console.

    *   Forgetting some punctuation. Does your if statement end with a colon? Are the parameters of your function separated by commas?

    *   Using too many, or not enough, quotation marks. In your editor, strings have a different color than the rest of your code. If you're missing a quotation mark, pieces of code will have colors that they shouldn't!

    *   Forgetting to close a bracket. Every opening bracket should have a matching closing bracket. Same thing with curly braces.

Look through your code for these spelling and punctuation mistakes. The more you practice, the easier it gets!

3. Next, check your indentation.

Python code is organized using indents. To put a line of code inside a for loop or an if statement, you start it with either one tab or four spaces. But you can't mix and match! If your indents use both tabs and spaces, you'll get an "IndentationError" in your code. If this happens, delete all your indents, then re-indent with either tabs *or* spaces.

4. Read over your code to see if there are any logic errors.

Maybe your program didn't crash, but you're not getting the results you should. We call this a logic error. Everything is spelled correctly, which means it's time to dig deeper for your bug!

Maybe you forgot to write a line of code. Maybe you put code inside a loop when it should be outside of a loop. Another very common mistake is to use the = sign (assignment operator) instead of the == sign (comparison operator).

Go through your code line by line. How does each line help the program achieve its goal? Are you missing a key step?

5. Finally, try adding print statements.

When you print a variable, you display its value in the console. Then, you can check if it's storing the value you want! Maybe you're expecting a string, but the variable contains an integer. Or maybe the list should have four elements, but it only has one. Once you've printed a variable, it's often clear how to fix your code. Tweak your program, run it again, and see if the value is now correct.

Print as many variables as you want. You can always delete these lines of code when you're done debugging. The values inside your variables may surprise you!

Here are some common coding errors you might make when starting out, and some quick fixes to get your code running smoothly again:

Error	What needs to be fixed?
NameError: name is not defined	<ul><li>You misspelled a variable name, or you forgot to define it.</li><li>You forgot to import a library or module.</li><li>You defined your variable, but too low in the program. Move the definition several lines up.</li><li>Your function is being called before it's defined. Always define your functions near the top of your code file!</li></ul>
SyntaxError: invalid syntax	You forgot an important symbol, like a colon or a comma. Check your functions, conditionals, loops, and lists for missing punctuation.
SyntaxError: unexpected EOF while parsing	You forgot to close a round bracket, square bracket, or curly brace.
SyntaxError: EOL while scanning string literal	The quotation marks surrounding your strings aren't in the right places—you might be missing one.
TypeError: unsupported operand type	You tried to add an integer to a string, add a Boolean value to a string, or multiply two strings. Maybe you forgot to convert a value or your variables are storing a value you didn't expect.
TypeError: missing required positional argument	Your function call is missing an argument.

Error	What needs to be fixed?
IndentationError: expected an indented block	You need to indent a line (or more) of code. Check all your if statements, for loops, while loops, and functions.
NameError: name "true" is not defined	You forgot to write a Boolean value (True or False) with a capital letter.
You're always skipping over a loop or a conditional	Your condition is always False. Check the values inside the variables used in your condition.
Your variable contains "None"	You forgot to return a value in your function.
Your code always runs the first branch of your conditional	You might be using the assignment operator (=) instead of the equals-to operator (==).

With these tips and tricks, you'll be a master bug hunter in no time!

Resources

Beanz Magazine (BeanzMag.com)

Beanz is a magazine about "kids, code, and computer science." It has educational articles and hands-on coding activities for kids ages 5 to 18.

BrainPOP.com

The BrainPOP website has a great section about computer science with videos, worksheets, games, and quizzes covering lots of different subjects.

CodeCombat.com

Learn Python by playing puzzle games! This is a great way to review your basics.

CodeWizardsHQ.com: Python for Kids

CodeWizardsHQ offers hands-on online classes for kids with a live instructor.

Computerphile

Computerphile is a YouTube channel about "computers and computer stuff." The channel has videos covering lots of interesting topics, from artificial intelligence to hacking to the history of computer science.

HackerRank.com

The HackerRank website has plenty of hands-on coding challenges. You can practice new coding languages or try writing games and algorithms.

HourofPython.com

The Trinket team has collected a series of free Python activities and challenges.

PyGame.org

PyGame is the most popular graphics library in Python. Check out the official PyGame website for tutorials to get you started.

TutorialsPoint.com

TutorialsPoint is a website that has a tutorial for everything. You can review the basics of Python or learn more advanced topics.

Tynker.com

Tynker.com has fun, engaging Python courses that are full of games and puzzles.

Glossary

algorithm: A series of precise, step-by-step instructions that solve a problem

and operator: A logic operator that joins two Boolean expressions into one mega-expression; both expressions must be true in order for the mega-expression to be True.

append: Add a new item to the end of a list

argument: A value inside a function parameter

assignment operator (=): Assigns a value to a variable; not to be confused with the equals-to operator (==)!

attribute: A variable that belongs to an object

Boolean: A data type for values that are either True or False

Boolean expression: A mathematical expression that uses variables, values, and comparison operators. Boolean expressions must be True or False.

bug: An error in the code; it could be a typo, a missing line of code, or a problem with the code's logic.

code editor/editor: The window where you write your Python code. Often, the editor is part of your IDE.

comments: Lines of text that are ignored by the program

compiling: Transforming human code into machine code (1s and 0s)

condition: A Boolean expression used in coding structures like while loops and conditionals; they can use both variables and values and are either True or False.

conditional: A coding structure that decides which lines of code are run and which lines are ignored

console: A window that displays a program's text output; users can also interact with a program using the console.

data structure: A tool to organize large amounts of data

data type: Determines what values the data can have, how much space it needs in a computer's memory, and how the data responds to different math operators like plus (+), minus (-), multiply (*), and divide (/).

debugging: The process of searching for a mistake in our code

dictionary: A collection of key-value pairs; the items of this data structure aren't ordered.

dummy value: A placeholder value used to start a loop or function; dummy values should be replaced by real ones as soon as possible.

editor: A special text editor used to write and edit code

equals-to operator (==): A comparison operator that returns True if two values are equal

f-string: A string that includes text and variables

file extension: A group of letters that appear after a file's name, like ".jpg" or ".py"; the file extension tells a computer about the file's format.

floating point number: A data type for decimal numbers, shortened to "float"

for each loop: A type of loop that can be used to access each item in a list, one at a time

for loop: A type of loop with a built-in counter; for loops only last for a set number of rounds.

function: A block of code that completes a specific task

IDE: Stands for "integrated development environment"; an IDE is a program that is used to edit and run code.

if-elif-else statement: A conditional structure with two or more branches

if-else statement: A conditional structure with two branches; one of the branches is always run by the program.

if statement: A conditional structure with a single branch

input: The information needed to start a program

integer: A data type for whole numbers, shortened to "int"

library: A folder full of code that contains useful helper functions; you can import them to use the functions in your code. One library might have several modules.

list: A data structure with ordered elements; it can also have repeat elements.

loop: A tool for repeating code

math operators: Symbols used inside math equations, like plus (+), minus (-), multiply (*), and divide (/)

method: A function that belongs to an object

module: A collection of specialized functions that can be imported and used in a program

not-equals-to operator (!=): A comparison operator that returns True when two values are different and False when two values are equal

not operator: A logic operator that flips the value of a Boolean expression so that True becomes False and False becomes True

object: A user-defined data structure with attributes and methods

or operator: A logic operator that joins two Boolean expressions into one mega-expression; at least one expression must be True in order for the mega-expression to be True.

output: The finished product of a program

parameter: A variable created to pass input to a function; parameters can only be accessed inside that same function.

printing: Displaying a text message in the console

running: Executing the instructions in a program, one line at a time

runtime: The time a program spends running

spaghetti code: Code that is disorganized and messy

string: A data type that stores text

syntax: The set of spelling and formatting rules for a programming language

text prompt: A sentence that tells the user what to do

tuple: A data structure with ordered elements; once created, the elements in a tuple can't be changed.

variables: Tools used to store the information inside programs

while loop: A loop that uses a condition; while the condition is True, the loop keeps going.

Index

About the Author

Patricia Foster is a software developer from Ottawa, Canada. Since graduating from Carleton University in 2017, she's tutored students, written for magazines, and contributed to books about programming. She's passionate about helping others discover their love of computer science. You can often find her drinking peppermint tea, petting a cat, or dancing in an elevator—though probably not all at once.